Facing the Mirror

EBONY STEWARD

EBONY STEWARD

Copyright © 2019 Facing the Mirror

by Ebony Steward

All scripture references are KJV unless otherwise stated.

Cover design by Kingdom Graphic Designs

Published by Destiny House Publishing, LLC.

Website: www.destinyhousepublishing.com

Email: inquiry@destinyhousepublishing.com

P.O. Box 19774

Detroit, MI 48219

All rights reserved.

ISBN-13: 978-1-936867-45-5

DEDICATIONS

I would like to dedicate this book first and foremost to God. Without him, I would be nothing; and without him, I wouldn't even be able to write this book. Secondly, I want to dedicate this book to the strong and beautiful women in my family. I want to say thank you to each and every one of you, Blanche Hines (Grandmother), Valerie Hines (Mother), and a host of aunts and cousins. You women have been in my life since I was born, and have all had a hand in helping me to become what I am today. Your solid foundation and intelligence is what I admire most in each of you. If I grow to be half of what you all are, I have become more than I could have ever dreamed. Thank you for being examples of classy women, and showing me how to be a lady. Thank you for keeping me grounded and in check when I needed to be. Thank you for loving me past my flaws and my mistakes. Thank you for seeing greater in me when I didn't see it in myself. To all of my uncles, especially Ted, Barry and Clee, thank you for showing me how a man should treat a woman. Thank you for every chair you ever pulled out. Thank you for every door you ever opened. Thank you for showing me what a protector is. Thank you for loving me like a man should. Thank you for treating me like a queen.

I would like to thank all of my church family, His Glory International Covenant Ministries. You guys are my second family and I love each of you, dearly. You all have supported me, and helped me through some of my toughest times in life. I know I can call all of you to pray and just to talk. You can't find those kinds of relationships everywhere. Trust me, I don't take it lightly. And last, but certainly not least, I want to dedicate this book to 2 men who meant the WORLD to me, my father, Lloyd James Steward, and my big cousin/brother, Rodney Wilson. Both of you have passed on now and it has been hard for me, but I know you're up in heaven being my guardian angels, even as I type this page. I want to say thank you for loving me and always being there. Thank you for every smile and every lecture. I would give anything to hear both of your voices right now. I love you all to the moon and back. Also, to my Uncle Sam who passed away not too long ago. I will always remember you for your one-of-a-kind jokes and personality. Your sense of humor could change the whole mood in the room and you will be truly missed... RIP my 3 angels.

CONTENTS

	Acknowledgments	i
1	Pushing Past the Pain	6
2	The Dating Game	53
3	Embracing Your Flaws	93
4	A Night Out Doesn't Mean Put Out	112
5	Sisterhood	130
6	The New You	154
7	Prophetic Release	162
	About the Author	166

Chapter 1

PUSHING PAST THE PAIN

"Bad things do happen; how I respond to them defines my character and the quality of my life. I can choose to sit in perpetual sadness, immobilized by the gravity of my life, or I can choose to rise from the pain and treasure the most precious gift I have life itself" -Walter Anderson

As a child, your life almost seems perfect. You have mom and dad to help guide you through life. There aren't really any major issues in your life because you are a child. The most you have to deal with is what cartoon character you want to perform at your birthday party.

As you get older, you start to realize that you aren't a little girl anymore. You start to see the world for what it really is. You start to ask questions about things that you normally wouldn't have cared about before. Some of you may have asked about your family background and found out you were adopted. Now that you know this information it sparks something in you and makes you want to find your biological parents for answers. You want to know who they are, and more importantly why they felt the need to give you away.

Also, some of you girls will have to deal with facing the fact that your dad doesn't play a significant role in your life that he should. He doesn't call enough, come and see you enough, or do anything for you. For a girl, it's very heartbreaking to not have that father- daughter relationship because you never really learn how to deal with men accordingly. Getting older is supposed to be fun. The older you get, the closer you are to becoming an adult and being in control of your own life. Sounds fun, right? You look forward to the big birthdays 13, 16, 18, and the most important of them all, 21.

In addition to the exciting parts of getting older you have to deal with the negative side of things. Having to face the truth about your life and where it's headed. You will never understand why things happen to you, but know everything does happen for a reason.

Growing up, I never really felt like I had the typical kid or "normal life". As an adult, I have vivid memories of living in the house where I grew up on the West side of Chicago. I remember the day we moved in the house. I remember it being such a good day because we all were excited! Now, looking back on things, I can now say that there were too many people living under one roof. When you have a lot of hands in the pot, something is bound to go wrong.

I lived in a home with my grandmother, my mom, an aunt, 2 uncles, 2 cousins and my brother. When I was younger I didn't think anything was wrong with this living arrangement, but as I got older I started to see and feel how toxic it was for all of us. Because certain ones didn't necessarily carry the responsibility of chipping in, the majority of everything fell on my mother and grandmother. This greatly affected my brother and I. My mother never really talked to me about her financial struggles, but I have always been a child with keen discernment. So whether she said it to me or not, I knew she and my grandmother both were stressed out a lot with the weight of carrying a household. It pained me to see my mom go through some of the things she endured while living in this house. My mom is like my bff so I never want to see her in pain or feel undervalued or unappreciated.

My mother is a passive person. She doesn't like drama or confrontation at all so she will take and take and take until she can't take any more for the sake of not having conflict. This made me angry and resentful towards her because when I would be ready to snap and say something for her, she would tell me to sit down and be quiet or stay in my place. I understood it because I was a pre-teen trying to fight my mom's battles for her, but only because I felt like she wouldn't. As a result, I adopted this "I'm not letting anybody disrespect or take advantage of my mom" mentality". It would only cause me problems down the line.

In my head, my thoughts were if you are footing the bill then you should be calling the shots. The thing that drove me most crazy was the fact that my mom didn't drive. We only had 1 driver in the house who was not a fan of driving that often. So when we wanted to go or do something, we had to go through this person. Sometimes you got a yes and sometimes you got a no. The 'no' response often made me mad for two reasons. One was because I wasn't able to do anything about it and 2 because my mom wasn't able to do anything about it.

We could never go on family trips to the movies, or bowling because if the driver didn't want to go, then we didn't have a way there. So a lot of things that I desired to do with my mom and brother never happened because of lack of transportation. As I continued to get older, I started to feel stuck and like I was in bondage living in this house. I didn't like the way things were being done. I didn't like the way the house structure was setup, and I didn't like feeling like I was suffering for mistakes that adults had made.

There were many nights in this house that I would wait for everyone to go to sleep. I would go downstairs, sit at the kitchen table and cry hoping that things would change, one day. I hoped that my life wouldn't always be like this, because I knew there was greater. I just didn't know how to get to it.

I spent a lot of time in mental torment in this house because I didn't have anyone to talk to about how I felt? I had some pretty strong feelings and opinions, but I knew if I were to share them I would hurt some of their feelings and that wasn't my intention. However, my feelings were hurt and to me it felt like no one cared.

I had witnessed my uncles being high on drugs. I saw my cousin drunk, and there was a lot of bickering and family arguments in the house. Every time someone would argue, once I was alone, I would break down and cry over it. I felt like I couldn't show my emotions. My mom was dealing with enough already, and my grandmother was too old to bother with this. I had nowhere to express myself, so I bottled it all up and dealt with it as best I could. That didn't turn out too well for me. I took on the burden of trying to make sure my mom was ok and not stressed, as well as the burden of wanting to help take care of things because I saw how heavy it was becoming on the both of them. I was a kid in school so there wasn't much I could do, but It was imprinted in my head to take care and be there for my mom. I couldn't do it financially, so I did it physically and emotionally.

On the other end of things, there was a piece of me that was resentful towards my mom because I felt like it was her fault for how life had panned out. I felt like if she would have taken some opportunities and made some different decisions then things would have been better for her my brother and I. I couldn't understand why my friend's parents were either working or had careers and my mom, at this point, couldn't work because she had a slipped disk in her back. It just felt like all of the odds were working against us.

Because there was so many of us under one roof, I never had the luxury of being able to have my own room. We slept 3 to a bed. I was against the wall, my little brother in the middle and my mother on the edge. For years, this is how we had to sleep and I hated it. I was a teenage girl and I felt like I didn't have space or any privacy. I remember being in school and my friends would ask could they come over after school. Because I had nowhere for them to come, I would lie and say that they couldn't come over. I told them I hadn't cleaned my room and my mom wouldn't allow it. I lied often about a lot of things because I was too embarrassed to tell my friends the truth. Sometimes there was tension in the house. Let's just face it being family didn't mean that we liked each other's decisions or actions, all the time. I felt like my mom, brother and I were the outcasts because my mom was the only one with kids that were active and very loud (in a good way lol). We actually wanted to get out the house and do fun stuff. So when we could never do anything, we were angry. Then we would hear the side comments of how we had bad attitudes and how my mom really needed to deal with us before we got out of hand. When in reality, it wasn't about having a bad attitude. It was about the fact that we were children who wanted to do normal kid things, that we couldn't. Adults forget that you have to make it a point to hang out with children and spend quality time with them. That's what I feel like we missed out on. I know if my mom would have had the money and actually knew how to drive, she would have been doing things with us. Unfortunately, she didn't and we suffered greatly.

I would often talk to God and ask him to help us out of this situation and to make it better. I never felt like he was listening to me because nothing ever changed. One day as an adult, I had a memory from childhood that let me know God was always with me, even in the early stages of my life. When I was living in that house and on those nights when I would sit at the kitchen table and cry, after I would go back upstairs to the room to lie down, an angel would come and grab me out of the bed and take me to the corner of the highest ceiling we had in the house. The angel would hold me and rock me to sleep and then when I would wake up it would be the next morning. When I was younger, I didn't know what it was. I would say something made me fly. Once I discovered that 'the something' was an angel, it made me feel bubbly on the inside; because no matter how bad the living experience may have been for me angels were always with me to comfort me and to hold me. Which reminds me of the scripture that says he (God) will never leave nor forsake you.

Now as if all of this wasn't bad enough, it gets a little deeper because little did I know my life was about to take a drastic change! I can remember it like it was yesterday, my cousins had just come to the states from Japan. My cousin, Brianna and I had gotten very close because I'm only 6 months older than her. We are like bff's and did not want to be apart from each other. I had gone to her house to stay for what was supposed to be a few days, but ended up being a day. Brianna's mom, Angie, which is my big cousin came down stairs and interrupted us playing and told me I had to go home, for some reason. Instantly Brianna and I both got angry and started questioning her and trying to figure out why I couldn't stay. Angie never really went into detail about it. She insisted that I couldn't stay and to gather my things so we could go back to my house, which was an hour away. I knew in my heart it had to be for something important because, who just wants to take an hour drive for the sake of it? I gathered my things and we were headed back to Chicago. I was angry, of course. Once we finally got to my house, I saw ALL of my family there and everyone was crying and looked so sad. I didn't say anything to anyone I came in and went to the bathroom but my emotions had changed at this point from anger to curiosity. As I was in the bathroom, I remember thinking that the only person I didn't see was my dad. In the back of my mind, I knew something had happened to him but of course I didn't want to think the worst. When I came out of the bathroom, I saw some aunts, my cousin, Angie and my mom; they had my younger brother with them and took us in my grandmother's room. My heart was racing because I knew something was going on. Lo and behold, I was correct something had happened to my dad. He had passed away of a heart attack in his sleep, the night before; which just happened to be 2 weeks after my 13th birthday. I instantly burst into tears and began to weep on my mother. Just a few days before this, my dad had picked up my brother and I from school and we went to get something to eat. We came back to my house and we all were sitting around the table and eating and laughing. I could not believe that I went from that little girl having a good time with her dad to this little girl who would never see her dad again. After a few days I had cried so much to where I didn't think I could get another tear out of me.

Before my dad died, I had never gone to a funeral before, so I didn't know what to expect. I knew people would be crying but I didn't know what the energy was going to be like or how everyone else was going to react. After a long week the day had come and it was time for the funeral. This was the *saddest* day of my 13 years on earth; having to walk up the aisle to a casket that my dad was sleeping in, knowing he would never wake up again. It was so bad for me that I couldn't even look in the casket. I came down the center of the aisle and I went to my seat because I didn't want to see my dad like that. My family had such nice things to say about my dad and it really helped to hear how many lives he had touched and that people genuinely liked him and his personality. I was crying so much that the letter I wrote to read, I couldn't even gather the nerve to read it. I asked my cousin to read it for me and she did. A few days after the funeral, I had time to think and reflect on what had just taken place. That was the last time I was ever going to see the man I called daddy.

Fast forward to 8 years later, I realized how traumatic that funeral was for me. I had all these emotions that I held in for 8 years and I finally released them in a conversation with my cousin. I was explaining to her that I don't remember anything that the pastor said from the eulogy. I didn't know who that man was and I wasn't even sure if he knew my dad or not. Since my dad's funeral I have unfortunately buried 3 other loved ones: 2 uncles and cousin. My cousin, Angie, did the eulogy at all 3 of them. She is an apostle and she knew them all. We were all family.

Listening to the words she shared and how she encouraged us all that we would see them again one day in heaven, made me feel like I could cope with the death. I know one day I will see their smiling faces. She sympathized with everyone and she made sure that they were celebrated even in their deaths. Normally when people have a funeral, it's a sad occasion. Everyone is around there moping and being depressed and balling their eyes out….you know the normal reactions. It's what I call a sad funeral. The funerals that my cousin, Angie eulogized were sad because we had just lost loved ones and of course we were hurt. The odd thing is that they didn't stay sad though, at some point during the funeral and her talking about their characters and all the things they had done, it dried our tears and we didn't feel so sad anymore. We started to remember the good times and smile through the tears and the hurt. We rejoiced in the fact that we would see them again.

I feel like my dad had a sad funeral, I didn't really know anyone on my dad's side of the family. They tried to comfort us as best they could, but they were not that affectionate. I don't ever remember the pastor who did the eulogy saying that we would see him again.

Now I'm a Christian so I believe that my dad is in heaven and that I will see him again. When I was 13 I didn't think like that. I wasn't as into church as I am now. So for years I cried at the fact that I didn't know if I was going to see my dad again or not. For years, I didn't even like to talk about my dad because all of these emotions were tied to him. I thank God for his grace and mercy because that's how I am able to write and tell the story today. At the repast I only remember really talking to my uncle and a couple of my half-brothers. But for the most part, I was with my mom's side of the family. It bothered me that I didn't really feel the love from everyone. I had just became a teenager and I could feel the lack of affection in the room. As I got older I was able to realize that my dad's family didn't grow up in the same way that I did. My family is super close and we are all in each other's business because we care. For other families, that's peculiar and doesn't make sense. It took me a long time to wrap my head around this because I just wanted the relationship with them. Another thing that bothered me was that 2 of my big cousins and my younger cousins didn't come to the funeral. For the life of me, I couldn't figure out why they didn't come. In my mind, I felt like it wasn't that important to them and that they didn't care about my dad as much as everyone else did. The younger cousins were my big cousin Angie's kids. Remember I said that my cousin Brianna and I were so close so I expected to have her to be there for me and she wasn't. I wanted to say something but I didn't want anyone to be mad or think I was being overly dramatic, so I suppressed it all those years. But when my uncle Sam died it was like the gate had opened and all these feelings came fluttering back. I knew I had to talk to someone and tell them all how I felt. I expressed myself to my cousin, Angie, whom I thank God for because she has been a rock for me many days. I told her that it hurt me that she didn't allow them to come to the funeral. She expressed to me that it wasn't anything intentional which I knew it wasn't. She said that she just didn't want to expose her kids to a funeral so young because they had never been to one. If I was 13 then her oldest which was Brianna was 12 so at the time her kids were all 12 and under. I understood her reasoning and she apologized and we moved on. She also suggested a great idea which was to have a memorial in my dad's honor to give me some new memories instead of the one I have now. That was the best thing I had heard that day. It made me feel like she completely understood where I was coming from and that I wasn't crazy for feeling how I did.

Now going back to after the funeral. I had to come to terms with my dad not being around to tell me I was beautiful and that he loves me. I didn't have that male figure in my life anymore to make me feel special and treat me like the queen that I was. My thoughts were that I never really got to say goodbye to him. We all know one day we are going to have to bury our parents, but not at the age of 13. It was such a terrible time for my family because my dad was a good man. He made sure that my brother and I were taken care of and my mom as well. He and my mom did not live together so he would come over all the time and spend time with us, laughing, talking, helping with our homework etc. He was the true definition of a good father.

One summer, I wanted to go to this summer camp thing in Maywood. My mom told me I couldn't go. She and my dad had made the decision together. I was so mad, I stayed downstairs and pouted. That's what we girls do. My dad asked my mom where I was, she said, "Downstairs; mad and pouting." So my dad called for me. I came upstairs and he asked me what was wrong with me. I told him I really wanted to go to this particular summer camp really bad. He told me ok and to stop pouting, that they would figure it out. And they did because I got to go to the camp.

Another time my cousin, Tamica wanted to take me to Florida with her and some of her friends. My mom didn't work because she was disabled, so the only income was my dad's and he made sure I was well taken care of, and was able to do everything I wanted. As I get older I'm able to remember these good times and use them to help me to cope with his death. Knowing that he would give the world for me, made me feel loved and protected. I respected my dad so much and the man that he was in our lives. Some fathers have kids and then they act like the child asked to be here. They don't feel a sense of responsibility to father the child or they think because the mother is around that the child is ok. When I was born my dad already had 4 children whom he fathered and cared for tremendously. They were all boys, and in my opinion, boys might be a bit more of a handful than girls…..Right ladies? By the time I came along, my dad could have been like, "Um no, I'm tired. You got this one by yourself. I have raised 4 kids already." He didn't say anything like that; he actually was overjoyed at the fact that he was having a little princess (me).

My dad was a real stand up kind of guy. He made sure that I wasn't around acting like a fast little girl. I remember coming home from school and telling him that I learned something in school and that I wanted to show him. He thought it was something educational, it definitely was not. It was a dance someone showed me. I bent over, put my hands on my knees and arched my back and I popped my booty. I can't even believe that that's something I thought he would be proud of, but I did. After I finished, I stood there and waited for his response which I thought was going to be good; but I'm sure you can guess it was a bad one. My dad in the loudest scariest voice said, "DON'T YOU EVER LET ME CATCH YOU DOING THAT AGAIN. DO YOU HEAR ME?" I got scared and quickly answered yes and according to my grandmother I cried....but of course I don't remember that part.

When I think about all of these things, although my dad isn't here anymore, it makes me very grateful for the time I did have him here with me. He wanted me to be a sophisticated woman and not run around popping my booty for people. He wanted me to respect myself enough to save that for my husband. Okkkkaaayyyy.

Most of you can't relate to losing a parent by death. If you haven't lost your dad, and he is still active in your life consider yourself one of the lucky ones. Never take it for granted. It's one of the most precious things in the world.

Some people are so consumed by life that they forget the little things such as putting in a phone call to their dad. We all get busy and things happen, but, never get so busy where you don't have time for your parents. I say all the time that I wish I could just call my dad and ask for his advice. If your dad is still living but not active in your life, I know you are affected by that in your day to day life. Who wouldn't be? It's the fact of knowing that you could do and be a part of my life but you CHOOSE not to. That sometimes can be a hard pill to swallow but you have to overcome the rough patches and use it to your advantage.

My worst fear for someone would be to lose a loved one and have any feeling other than love towards that person. If you have anger, hate, bitterness etc., it will make the passing all the more difficult for you because, you have to deal with the guilt. The guilt comes from not being able to say, 'forgive me', 'I forgive you', 'I'm sorry' or 'I accept your apology'.

If your dad isn't in your life by your own choice, I advise you to fix whatever the situation is and make it right. You don't want to wait till it's too late to realize that you have wasted all this time being angry... and for what?

If you can relate to losing a father, you have to know that I felt sick to my stomach and abandoned. It's almost like something in you changes when you lose a parent. I felt different I felt open. I didn't have the protection that I once had before. I felt like if I was going to have to fight, I was fighting by myself and for myself. I attacked people because I was hurting and I thought that I had to get people before they got me. I developed a trust issue, it was difficult for me to trust people who weren't family or close friends.

When you hear your parents saying to you that they will never leave you, you believe them. Although we know it's not true because we all die at some point. Something in us makes us believe that they will never leave us, so when they do it's almost like a letdown. As crazy as it sounds, these were my true feelings at the time. I felt like at this point, my guard was down. Anything and anyone that wanted to come in my life and do good or evil could have. I like to be in control and have control over things so for me to feel like this it was overwhelming. I didn't have the wisdom then that I have now. I didn't know that it was really the devil plotting to use this situation against me in the end. The devil is not remorseful at all. He sees you down and he will pick up his foot and place it on your back to make sure you stay down. He doesn't want you to get up, and learn better, and try to do better. He likes us broken, crying, and just utterly confused. The devil sees that as open grounds to come in and try and tell you, "Girl, what you got to live for, huh? Yo' daddy done died. Life ain't gone never be the same. Just kill yourself so you can be with him." The enemy is smart and he takes advantage of us when we are broken and when he can get to us. He takes those moments and run with them. But when you have some praying family members, the devil can't do nothing with you. He will try and make you believe him. But when people are praying for you, God will stand for you and say, "Not so, Devil. Take your hand off my daughter." At that moment, I didn't know how to feel. All I could do was cry my eyes out and find comfort in my family and friends. Losing any parent for me would have been hard; but for me to be a girl and lose my father was very detrimental to my life. A father has a very special place in a girl's heart. He is the first man she will ever love who will love her back. He is the first man that will open the door for her. He is the first man that will pull her chair out for her, and waits for her to sit down. He shows her how to be able to detect the difference in a good man and a player. He tells her how not to belittle a man and to let him be the lead. He teaches her how to be in a non-sexual verbally intimate relationship with someone. He pours into her so that she can grow up and know exactly what to look for in a husband. What happens when there is no father to pour into her life and she doesn't know what to look for in a man? She has to grow up and figure it out as she goes. That can be scary. You're going into the situation blind. You are a girl, how can you know what a man wants? You don't know that there are times you have to let your guard down and be subject to certain things, because all mom taught you was to be a strong woman.

The majority of the time, she is lost and finds a man; but definitely not the right man. Often times he is someone who reminds her of her dad. For that reason alone, she will stick around because her heart is in pain from her own loss. Also, she doesn't know what her worth is, so she tends to let the world define it for her. The world defines her as the thing that gets her the most attention, or the thing that they think is her best quality, such as big boobs or a big butt. She will put this attribute on display at all times because it's the thing that gets her the attention she needs and wants from a man. Her standards are low and she settles for anything that comes her way, good or bad. If she is lucky enough to end up with a good guy, she will run him away with her insecurities and her low self-esteem. A man wants a strong confident woman to stand by his side. How can she if she doesn't even know what attracted him to her in the first place?

When I was 13, I wasn't allowed to date. My mom was very strict and wouldn't even allow me to talk on the phone to boys. Like any normal teenager, I snuck and did it anyway. My trick was to have my cousin, K.J. call the house and ask for me he would then have the guy on 3 way. (It always amazed me how we seemed to never understand math and science but could always scheme around our parents). The type of guys I liked were the ones who were cute, but typically didn't have an ounce of respect for me. Often times they were talking to other girls. I never liked to be cheated on or "played". When I found out, I would stop talking to them, and went looking for another. This was my first problem - looking for a boy to talk to. The Bible says when a man finds a wife he finds a good thing. I wasn't looking to be married because I wasn't even allowed to date. I still shouldn't have been looking for anything. If someone wanted to talk to me they should have come to find me, not the other way around. Because of what I had been through, I had a desire to be loved, liked, and wanted by a boy. I didn't like to be alone or restricted from dating. I thought what I was feeling was normal and that all girls felt like this, but that wasn't the case. My desire to be needed stemmed from not having a dad. I simply did not know what to do with the hurt and pain that I was feeling. A few family members suggested counseling, but I turned it down because I felt that it would make me weak. I am probably one of the most sensitive people in the world. I literally cry over anything. I remember watching an episode of Criminal Minds and one of the agent's wife died. I started crying, and I mean crying like it was my mom that had died. So I knew if I went to counseling they were going to have me in there crying and getting in my feelings. I didn't want that. I was trying to be ok on my own. Actually, I should have accepted the counseling. It could have saved me a lot of heartache over the years. Sometimes as young girls, we think we know exactly what is best for us. If we stop, think and be completely honest with ourselves, we could see that we don't know as much as we thought. Teenagers are still children that need guidance. I can vividly remember my mom stepping up and playing both roles mom and dad to my brother and I. Still for me that wasn't enough to help me get over the loss of my dad. She could only help me with so much.

When I got older, about 16 or 17 and actually allowed to date, I longed so bad to be in a relationship. I felt something was wrong with me because now, I had no one to date. All of my friends were dating and in relationships and I was standing looking like the odd ball trying to figure out where my dude was. Thankfully I never found him and I'm glad I didn't. It wasn't until my adult years that I realized why God wouldn't allow me to meet anyone then. I was in a vulnerable place and didn't even realize that being alone was exactly what I needed at the time. Being alone was necessary for my healing and grieving process. Who knows the things I would have done at the time? My mind wasn't right because I was still hurting. I wasn't thinking like the normal Ebony. I was thinking like the Ebony that had just lost her dad and didn't know how to deal with her emotions. If I had met a boy at that time I could have possibly had sex and became pregnant or even worse caught an STD. Boys don't care how they get the sex, they just want it, even at the age of 13. Don't be fooled by age In this day and age, it is literally just a number.

When you have a lot going on in your life, it's very therapeutic to have a time of solitude. During this time you can allow your mind to roam freely and think about whatever the situation is that has you feeling as you are. There are times in life where you can postpone dealing with things. There are also things that you can't postpone. That thing will resurface constantly, and that's the thing that needs your attention. You don't want to let it linger until you find a different way of handling it. Unfortunately this is the mistake a lot of people make. They turn to drugs and alcohol to make themselves feel better. "When I'm high I don't have a care in the world", or "I'm going to drink my pain away". Any of those sound familiar? People think that these are real cures to easing pain. It's so ignorant to think this way. It's actually causing more pain.

When you are high and drunk, of course you don't have any care in the world. Your mind is so out of touch with reality. You probably do feel good for a few hours just drinking and getting high. But what happens when the high and the hang over wears off? You wake up with the exact same truth that you went to sleep with, the only difference you feel even worse than you did. Drinking and smoking only adds to the issue. It makes you want to keep doing it over and over for those few little moments of what you think are pleasure. You keep getting high to not be able to feel the pain of losing a loved one. You keep getting drunk to forget the pain you felt looking into the eyes of uncle "so and so" who molested you. You keep getting high to hide the pain of not feeling good enough, physically. Trying to hide the pain isn't the way to not feel it. In order to heal, you must deal with it and face it head on. Turning to drugs and alcohol is not the answer.

I tried for so long to not deal with the truth of my dad's death. When it came up in conversation, I would often change the subject. I couldn't stand to talk about it.

My real truth was that I had a lot of regrets when my dad passed away. I had prayed and wished that I had done so many things differently. My dad had 6 children, 5 boys and 1 daughter. As the only girl, I definitely should have spent more time with him while he was here. As girls, we want to get our nails and hair done, we want to shop until we drop. Men on the other hand could care less about all of that stuff. They want to play basketball and watch sports all the time. We girls start to feel like we have nothing in common with them. My dad was very into nature. He would go by the lake fishing and stuff like that. I was a girl so I didn't want to go by a lake or catch any stinking fish. I never went fishing with my dad before, but some of my older brothers had. I think I should have just taken the opportunity to spend time with him and gone fishing. I shouldn't have cared about where it was or what he was doing. I should have just been content that I was just simply spending time with my daddy. These are the things that we miss out on as kids, because we think we'll have our parents forever. We take them for granted and assume we'll have other opportunities to spend time with them. This is what made losing my dad so difficult. It made me feel like I had missed out on so much and the guilt from that is what I couldn't handle.

There are always going to be things that come up in your life that make you feel like "I regret that decision" or "I should have did this and that", but at the end of the day there is absolutely nothing you can do about it. You can't carry that burden of what you could have done. What's done is done. You have to let it go and move on. It's not healthy to walk around carrying so many burdens. Psalm 55:22 says "take your burdens to the Lord" He wants to bear our burdens. This is the awesome thing about God. He says to us, his children, "Come to me and give me your cares and you burdens let me carry all of them for you so that you can be free." None of us deserve God's grace, but he gives it to us anyway because he loves us with a pure heart. The burdens are too heavy for our physical bodies to try and carry. They will weigh you down and make you sick physically and mentally. It wasn't actually until I made peace with my dad in the spirit that I began to feel a little better. God has the power to change things here in the natural and in the heavens. I had some things that I needed God to change and work out in me with my dad. Since I couldn't physically call my dad, I called on God to start to do the work for me. One night, I prayed that God would take away the pain and fill the void in my heart for my dad. . When you lose someone it leaves you feeling empty inside like a piece of you has been taken, because it has been. I also prayed for God to help me and guide me in the steps of being ok with where my life was at the moment. I needed God to deal with this fatherless girl who was lost mentally, spiritually, and emotionally. In my time of prayer, I also prayed that God would deal with the resentment I felt towards Him. I didn't understand why he took my dad when there were so many other dead beats around. When things like this happen, initially a person gets upset and starts to question God about why he took their parent or why this and that is happening in your life? Some might question why they were even born, because it seems like there is so much chaos and a life of hardships. You get through one thing and then here comes another thing trying to take you down. Or they feel like they take 2 steps forward and get pulled 20 steps backwards. It's tough, but I know that God doesn't put more on us than we can bear. If your struggles are great then your destiny and the calling on your life is great, as well. The enemy will try and make you think you can't handle what is being thrown at you but that's only because he can see what you mean to God and he wants to try and destroy you before you see it yourself. Believe it or not, the devil will even use your own hands to destroy you. He doesn't care how you get destroyed as long as you do.

I'm not going to lie and tell you it was easy and I changed overnight, because I didn't. I went to sleep after praying and woke up feeling the same exact way I had been feeling. But I had to have faith and believe that God had mended my relationship with my dad and I, and he had begun to work on me like I asked Him.

I just hadn't started to work on myself. I wanted God to do all the work for me. It was crazy for me to sit back and think God was going to miraculously fix me, and I wasn't going to have to do anything. If I wanted to change I had to go after it. I couldn't sit and wait for it to come to me, because it wasn't. It's almost like wanting to be a model but not ever going to get pictures taken to build a portfolio. You have to take the necessary steps to getting what you want. I wanted change in my life so I first had to change the way I thought about myself. I wanted change so I couldn't act like a fatherless little girl. I had to act and behave like I knew God was my father and he would be all the man I needed. What did that look like in the natural? It meant that I was not trying to be in a relationship. I was ok with being alone. It also meant that I would not be looking for love in all the wrong places.

In that same way, you have to be able to see yourself changed and see yourself in a new light. To know that you can do better than what you have been doing is going to be encouragement to you. If you start to create standards for yourself, you will feel great. But don't fall short of them..

My older cousin Tamica told me about a prayer she prayed, that God would cover her from any guy that didn't mean her any good to her. I started to really think about if I wanted to pray this prayer or not because I knew that this would be one that He answers. I remember praying it. I am one that hates to waste time. I would hate to be talking to somebody that can't add something to my life. That's just a waste. So I prayed and as I suspected God answered my prayer...

I grew up on the Westside of Chicago. If you are familiar with the area, you know there is a store on every corner and boys hanging on those corners. My mom was so over protective that she normally didn't allow me to walk the streets to go anywhere. But if I wore her out enough, she would give in. So I guess this day I had worn her out. I was walking to the store to get some junk food. It was around the block where I knew for a fact that guys were standing on the corner. I looked cute so I just knew that someone was going to try and talk to me or ask me for my number. I walked in and bought my stuff, paid, and left I walked out and absolutely nothing. It was as if no one noticed me. Now for a few seconds, I was baffled about it. No one said anything to me. As I was walking back, in my head, literally I was talking to myself about it. I had to quickly remember, I was trying to change and remind myself of the prayers I prayed. I quickly came to myself and remembered that my goal was not to act as I had before.

For all of you that can relate to what I am saying, please know that it is definitely ok for you to make mistakes. I would be lying if I said it was going to be a walk in the park. You are going to be tempted by whatever floats your boat. That simply means that if you like tall, dark, and handsome men, then I can almost bet you every tall, dark, and handsome brother is going to come your way and want to talk to you. God will test you. He will show you what areas you are growing in and what areas still need work.

At the same time, the devil is always lurking to trip you up. He wants to get in your head and tell you that you can't change, or that you aren't growing. If you mess up, he'll tell you that God won't forgive you. Those are the times that you have to go straight to God and pray that God will strengthen you in times of weakness. The goal is to make progress and keep putting forth effort to becoming a better person and dealing with whatever situation you face. If you fail, then get back up. Repent to God and keep it moving. It doesn't help for you to linger on it. Address the mistake and figure out how you aren't going to do that the next time. This is how you grow in the natural and in the spirit.

After so long, I had accepted the fact that God had kept his word to me and he had kept me covered from any guy who didn't mean me any good. I had become very grateful that he kept me, especially as I watched everyone else around me go through so much with their no good boyfriends. I was very proud of myself for finding strength to be able to stand on my decision. It wasn't easy, but it was the best thing I could have done for myself and the beginning of what made me the person I am today.

As I continue to get older I continue to get stronger and stronger in my situation. Is it still hard for me when the anniversary of the death of my dad comes around? Yes, it is. Even on my birthday I think about it and on holidays; but I don't get depressed about it as I did before. I can talk openly about my dad to people now and not feel bad or any guilt about anything. I never will forget my dad but I'm able to think of him in a different light now. God has brought me a long way from where I used to be. I haven't ever really had a serious boyfriend and I am still waiting for God to bless me with that person. I'm not looking for any man. The right man will have to find me. I feel like everything I went through in this situation is going to help me to help someone else.

There are some of you whose dads aren't dead, they just haven't been in your life by choice. This is for you as well. These situations still apply to you because you are still missing the male figure in your life. You still have a void, because he just isn't around, and there's nothing you can do about that. Also, it can cause you to question why? What's wrong with you that he doesn't want to be around? I think having a living father and he not being present is more hurtful than him passing away. It's the choice in the situation that will make you angry and bitter. It's different if a person can't do because they absolutely can't be there. But if they are alive and healthy and not trying, it puts a new perspective on the situation. It can cause a person to not feel loved. As a result, they will soon look for the love in another man. If the dad would have just been the man and accepted his responsibilities your life could have turned out a lot different. Don't ever think it is your fault because it's not. You didn't ask to be here and you can't make a grown adult do what they are supposed to do. It's his loss that he doesn't want to step up and do things a father is supposed to do. He misses out on all the milestones in your life such as your graduations, getting married and having a relationship with his grandchildren. Sooner or later he will realize it, and by then he can only pray that God gives you the strength to forgive him. Let God be all that you need him to be to you. Let him minister to your heart. I promise you he will do just what you ask him to do.

    You might be in a situation where your mom is the absentee parent in your life. There are certain things you can get from your dad, but because he is a male, he can only show you so much. Then there is the time in your life when you need a mother. As a girl, having a relationship with her mom is very important , as well. Mom is the one who teaches you how to get and keep a man. Mom teaches you about letting that man know how to respect you, not treat you. There's a difference in the two. Mom is the one that will tell you if he doesn't stop when you say no, then you are to leave. If he calls you out your name to check him. She will also teach you to not run around with a lot of men period. Mom will tell you to clean your room because don't no man want a dirty woman. The relationship with mom and her daughter is one that should be open. At the same time, the daughter knows how far to go.

My mom and I are connected at the hip I consider her to be my best friend. I feel like if I can't go to my mom and tell her anything who can I go to? I thank God for the relationship with my mom because I know most girls don't have that relationship, and it's something that I do not take for granted.

Our moms have the role of teaching us how to become young ladies, self-respect, sex education, feminine hygiene, and how to take care of your household when you get older. Your mom is supposed to be your best friend when you are younger. I personally couldn't imagine not having my mom in my life. She taught me so much about how to love and respect myself as a lady. There's a difference in having respect and then having self-respect. Having respect is not cursing in front of elders, not talking back to your parents, or not behaving negatively with your teachers. But self-respect is not letting your girlfriends or guy friends call you bitches and hoes. Self-respect is not allowing any man to disrespect you. It is is loving yourself enough to make sure that your name is clean in the streets. Some girls can have a guy call them a hoe and not even be able to speak up and say, "You can't call me that because, I'm not a hoe." Their name is so ruined in the streets that they have no choice but to accept the roles they have set for themselves. My mom taught me early not to ruin my name, and to keep it clean. I was the girl who was always able to say, "You can call me stuck up or Goody Two Shoes, but what u can't call me is a Hoe (Thot in modern language); because that I was not."

If you're in this situation, I know it can be difficult, but you have to find another mother figure. I'm sure there is an aunt or older cousin you can talk to that can help you to become the wonderful lady, I know you can be. We have to learn how to take the situation and make the best of what we have around us, and use that to our advantage. I love that saying "if life gives you lemons, make lemonade". It is so true. Yes, life will be hard and difficult at times but you have to learn to squeeze that lemon until all the juice is out of it. If your mom wasn't there for you, as you needed her to be, forgive her and move on. Make the decision that you will not be that way with your own child. You can give your child something you never had and break the curse of not having a mother. Teach and show her the things your mother didn't, so that she can give them to her child when the time comes. The most important thing is to forgive your mother because, you can't do better than her if you're still harboring the pain of what she didn't do for you. You will take that into your adulthood, and become bitter and pass it down to your own children and then the cycle continues. You don't know how your mom's childhood was and even if her mom played a significant role in her life. If she didn't, then that's why your mom can't give you the love, affection, and attention you need, because she didn't get it.

Iyanla Vanzant from Fix My Life did a piece on Evelyn Lozada. I love me some Evelyn, but the thing that stuck out to me most was when Iyanla brought In Evelyn's mom. They were talking about what Evelyn saw as a child and how her mom grew up. The thing was Evelyn's mom had been given up when she was younger and her mom never really learned how to show love or receive it properly. So therefore she couldn't give it to Evelyn properly either which is why she was so quick to snap and be angry all the time. If your mom didn't receive it how can she give you something she never had herself? We as children always look at what our parents don't give us but we don't take into consideration their side of the story. . We have to be fair and a lot more understanding to them because some of our parents are giving us the best that they can.

Months after my dad passed away, I was still working on myself. I started dealing with a lot of rejection that I was getting from my dad's side of the family, especially my 4 step brothers. They are all a lot older than I was. I get that while I was grieving over the loss, they were too. But I felt like they could have been doing a lot more to spend time with me, especially because I am their only sister. For a little while one of my brothers came around to check on my younger brother and I to make sure we were ok. Then one day things started changing for the worse. When my dad was alive, my step brothers and I really didn't have a relationship. I would see them whenever I did, which wasn't very often. I always felt a bit of resentment towards my dad when he passed away because I thought he could have made sure we all were really a part of each other's lives. When he passed away, I just thought it would bring us all closer together; because we got to see that life is short and isn't promised. But instead I got the exact opposite. I have not had any type of relationship with my brothers my whole life. I am 25 years old and I can count on my hands the number of times I have seen them. I was 13 when my dad passed away and some of them were young as well; but they all were way older than me. So I feel like they should have made a bigger effort to make sure we all stayed in contact with each other. I was a kid. I didn't know anything about keeping a family together. I would try and reach out and keep in contact with them all, but it became a one-sided relationship. I felt as though I was the only one that cared about us having a relationship and getting to know one another at all! Once I figured out in my head that they were not going to be in my life as I had hoped, I started to build up a wall to shut them out. I tried to erase them from my memory because when I thought about it, it would make me angry. I didn't want to walk around angry and upset all the time, so I had to let them go. Little did I know I really hadn't let anything go, the rejection and disappointment still lived in me. If people would ask me about them, I would say I didn't care about them or that I had only 1 brother, my younger brother. If I kept telling myself I had only 1 brother, then I would start to believe it eventually, right? I had tried to mentally block them out of my life because I felt like they had physically and mentally blocked me out of theirs. The hurt and pain that I felt from this was very real. It made it difficult for me to let people in and to build relationships because I didn't like the feeling of being rejected. I developed the whole "I'm going to get you before you get me mentality". So if I did let you in, then you wouldn't be fully trusted because I didn't know what your motives were. All the while I was dying inside. I was trying to walk around and act like I was ok, like my step brothers not being in my life didn't affect me. When in reality, it absolutely did. I would look at TV and if I saw a show that had a little sister and a big brother, I would think about it. If I knew girls who had good relationships with their older brothers, I would think about. I might have even been jealous, because in my head I'm thinking will that ever be my life? Will my brothers ever want to build a relationship with me? I always wanted to be able to have my brothers meet my boyfriend and give him the third degree because my dad wasn't here to do it. I wanted brothers that would be so protective of me and if I had a problem I could call them. I wanted the little sister-big brother relationship so bad. If people didn't know the truth already, I would lie and tell them I had a great relationship with my brothers. I would tell them we hang out and that they had met my guy friends. Through my lies, I was screaming out for their attention, but I never got it.

One day, I got a phone call and it was from one of my brothers. He was telling me he thinks that my dad, he, and I were at fault for the relationship between my brothers not being as it should have been. I got so angry I started to cry. How dare you try and pin your faults off on me? I was 13 years old, and by the time I turned 18, I had made myself not care anymore. So I wasn't trying to reach out to them. I thought I was ok with not having a relationship with them. Now, I am very much my dad's child and I don't hold back my tongue for anyone. So I told him I thought he was wrong and that they all were wrong because they were the older ones who should have stepped up. We didn't see eye to eye and the conversation ended there. We didn't speak for a while. Then he called me again and said that he would come get me from my aunt's house so that we could go sit down and talk. I'm sure you can guess, that never happened.

It was incidents like this that made me want to never speak or see them again. I felt like I kept getting my hopes up only to be let down again, and I was tired of that feeling. I had to come to the conclusion that I can't make them do anything they don't want to do. Everyone goes through things in life. Sometimes they can't care about your needs because they have too much going on. So, now that I am a lot older I get it and I had to let it go. I couldn't carry around the anger and the rejection from them because, when God is ready to send someone into my life, I don't want to shut him out due to my issues with my brothers. Also, it wasn't healthy for me to worry so much about something I couldn't change. It was extra stress I didn't need to carry. You have to be able to confront these things because I promise you they will surface in areas you never thought. Honestly, I never thought that because I didn't have a relationship with my brothers that it would make it hard for me to receive and trust people. But it did, and I don't want to be labeled as that person. So for myself, I had to forgive and let go. I have given the situation to God and when he sees fit, then the relationship with my brothers will come.

I recently attended a powerful conference called Wounded Warriors. The conference was about restoration, and restoring the people of God who had been wounded by their situations and struggles. If we all are supposed to be warriors for Christ, we can't war if we are weighed down by our own stuff. It's like me having rejection issues, and then meeting someone with rejection issues and trying to bring them out, when I haven't even figured out how to bring myself out. Even as I write, it sounds funny. That would really be the blind leading the blind. I had to be able to get in a place where I could talk to God and tell him, "Look God, I am hurting and I know I am no good to you, if I don't overcome this battle. How could I help advance the Kingdom of God if I can't even face my own issues?" Because if I can't face mine then I most certainly can't stand with you and face yours.

The speaker at the conference said that it takes courage to be able to talk to God and ask him to touch these places in our lives; because they are so personal and it hurts to even think about. If I can't even think about it without getting angry, why would I want to deal with it for real? Who knows how I'll feel after I'm done. Often times we try to hide these emotions and cover up this part of our lives because it's almost embarrassing to tell people that we suffer and struggle in certain areas. I didn't like telling people that I felt rejected because my brothers weren't in my life, and that it made it hard for me to build relationships with people. I would treat people with attitudes for no reason and I would chalk it up to that's just my personality. But it wasn't my personality. God didn't create me like that. He created me to love people but because of my stuff I couldn't even operate in that. I was blocking what God was trying to do in life because of shame and thinking people were going to look at me crazy. But just as I was going through my stuff, someone else was going through the same thing. Just like me, she was afraid to talk about it. God wants to use us for his kingdom and to help bring souls to Christ. We can't do that whole heartedly if we aren't right. You don't want to be the reason someone misses their blessing or breakthrough because you wouldn't let God heal your wounds. Whatever yours may be, I dare you to allow God to touch that place. Let Him touch the thing only you know about, and the thing that troubles you when you think about it. Invite Him to touch the thing that makes you cry at night when you lay your head on your pillow, or the thing you feel embarrassed to tell anyone about. Let God come in and touch that place in your life. I promise you He will meet you there and show you how much he loves and cares about you. He will take that pain away from you. He died on the cross so that you wouldn't have to feel that burden, let alone carry it. He wants to help you. So allow him to do just that with whatever it is.

    The positive part out of the situation is that I ended up

building a great relationship with my Uncle Clee, on my dad's side. When my dad passed away, my uncle made it his business to come and spend time with my brother and I. He would take us to the movies, and out to eat One time he took us to downtown Chicago. It wasn't so much the things that he was doing that I liked, it was the fact that even in his grieving, he made time for us. He knew I was a girl who had just lost her dad and to me he stepped up and played that role for me. I will call him and talk to him about anything because I know that I can. He won't judge me, and he gives great advice. He always tells me that he is proud of me and that he knows my future is bright. It's those little things that matter the most to me. To know that he will be there when I need him and not miss the major events in my life is something special because I don't have my dad here. It makes me feel like a piece of my dad will always be around because of my uncle.

Once I was able to semi get through the hurdle of losing my dad and all the emotions that came with that, I started to feel oppressed with weights and burdens that I shouldn't have been carrying. I told you before that I adopted a mentality that I had to take care of and be there for my mother, at all times. I didn't know how bad it had got until we moved to Lake County and we were staying in our own house, finally. It was my mother, brother and I. I thought that we had finally gotten a break in life because now we had our own house. Everything was going good for a while, and then it was like all hell broke loose. Every other day, it was something new.

I was so elated when I had finally gotten a job, because I would be making some money. Then I realized I didn't have a vehicle so I had no way to get to work. I had to depend on someone else to get me there. My cousin stepped up a lot to help get me to work and I was so appreciative of her for that. However, in her helping me I realized I had a pride problem. I didn't like asking her to take me. I worked at Target and my shifts included Sundays. My cousin is the pastor and on Sunday, my family went to church. So on Sundays I would call off sometimes because I didn't have a way to get there and I wanted to be in church. Not having a car really started to affect me in such a way that it depressed me. The more I had to depend on other people, the more I got depressed. I felt like I was becoming a burden on everyone. As if taking me to work wasn't enough, when my mom needed to go to the store, we had to call my cousin or a family friend. At the time, the family friend and I could not see eye to eye about anything; but she and my mom were close. So when my mom would call her, sometimes I was ok with it and sometimes I would get mad. In my own jacked-up brain, I felt like she would think she was doing us a favor and that we would owe her something. I never wanted people to be able to throw anything in our face that they did for us. So sometimes if we needed to go to the store, we would walk to the Dollar General that was around the corner and down the street. The bad thing about this was my mother had a bad back and the walking wasn't good for her, but in tough times you do what you have to do. The entire time I worked at my job, I didn't have a car. And I ended up only working there for 3 months. They fired me after my 90 days, for having too many call offs. My issue was transportation. I remember hearing the HR lady tell me that it was my last day. I called my mom and cried my eyes out. I was so hurt. Of all the things to get fired for, who wants to hear you got fired for basically not having a car. My heart was so broken. I remember being angry and crying for days because I loved my job. My emotions were all over the place and the devil was for sure playing with my head. I remember going to my room, crying. I called my cousin. I told her that I was starting to lose hope in everything and that I didn't see why I should still be alive. Now I know some of you will say that I was being dramatic, but if you ever feel like nothing in your life is going right and for every 2 steps you take forward, you must take 30 back, then you will feel the same way. Remember I was also living with my brother. At the time, he was a troubled youth, that my mother nor I could control. My brother had decided that he wanted to be responsible for his own life and that he would not listen to my mother or me. I didn't have any kids, but I considered myself to be a disciplinarian but my mom is kind of not. My mother is a nurturer and she doesn't really discipline until she really has to. By this time, my brother was already out of control. Some days he was good. Other days he and I would literally argue all day, because I didn't like how he treated our mother. This is when I realized that I was so overly protective of my mother, because it made me start to really not like him. It wasn't really him that I didn't like. I didn't like his ways and his actions. I felt like we had already lost our dad and I wasn't going to let him kill my mom by stressing her out or causing her to have a stroke from screaming and yelling at him. I tried talking to him and verbally threatening him. Nothing worked. I remember asking my mom to put him out. Of course, she wouldn't do that. In my heart, I didn't really want her to but I wanted him to get his act together.

My brother ended up linking up with the wrong people and he wounded up in trouble multiple times with the police for petty offenses. But since we lived in Lake County, they didn't play with all the police calls and disturbing the peace. Because my brother could never get his act together, the village of that area decided to put us out of our home. We had to move in with my cousin and her family. Again, I was so sad and angry. Once you have experienced living in your own home, you never want to have to go back to living with someone else again. We had no choice but to pack up everything and move, and that's what we did. You would think that after all this, my brother would have gotten his act together. He did not. He continued to find trouble and hang out with the wrong crowd. The only difference was that the police were being called to my cousin's home instead of our old address.

My cousin is the pastor, so she was not used to having all the arguing and fighting in her house or not having peace when she wanted it. I started to feel the pressure of being a burden again. My cousin knew that we had nowhere else to go, so she took as much as she could from my brother before she told my mother he could no longer stay in her home. My mother wasn't going to let my brother live on the streets, so if she was kicking him out she was, in a way, kicking us all out. If my mom left I wasn't letting my mom go alone. So the actions of my brother yet again had us homeless, and basically I couldn't handle it. So again, I felt like my life would never change because it had been a mess for years, already. The thoughts of suicide came back to me, again. This time I really felt like why should I live? There was nothing I could do to change anything. I had no money and neither did my mom, at least not to move into another home. We were stuck with no options. it pained my heart to have to watch my mother go through so much because I knew she blamed herself for most of it. I saw her slowly throw in the towel and let depression sink in. It was obvious that she felt like she had no more options. She didn't even know if the situation would ever get better. I remember having a family meeting. Everyone was saying that they would allow me and my mother to come and live with them, but that my brother could not come because he had burned all his bridges with people. I know for my mom this was hard because no matter what he did, he was still her son and she didn't want to see him on the street with nowhere to go. This only made me want to take care of her and be there for her even more! I had never seen my mom cry so much in life. I remember telling her that we would be ok and that if we had to go live in a shelter, then that's what we would do together.

Living in a shelter was something that I prayed we would never have to do. But I know my mom felt like her options were gone and so did I. Thankfully, God had a plan. Another one of my cousins allowed my mother and I to live with them. My brother went to stay with my 2 of my uncles. As I look back on all these events, this was a very trying and dark time in my life. I truly thank God for still being in my right mind. I know for sure I should have had a mental or emotional breakdown because there was a lot of pressure. I felt responsible for my mother and my brother. I knew it had gotten to be too much for my mother to handle. So I decided to take it on and I regretted it from the moment I did. We were never designed to carry burdens. That's what God is for. He says to exchange our burdens for his yoke, because it is easy. The devil knows we aren't intended to carry half of the things that we do. He plays on that. In the times you are overwhelmed, you feel like it's easier to be alone, left in the dark or even kill yourself. I felt all of these things because I was just tired and I lost hope in everything, even God. I didn't understand how he could love me so much, yet have us going through all that we did. I remember some days when we were living in our own house, we didn't even have food! One time, we had to heat up some left over holiday food from a few weeks prior. It was in the freezer. So we spread it between the 3 of us.

As I write this, it brings tears to my eyes because I see how far God has brought us. It hasn't been an easy journey and there were several bumps along the way. But I can say, I am one of the ones that made it; because someone didn't. Someone actually listened to that voice that told them to kill themselves, and someone actually had a mental break down. I thank God for his hand being on my life, even when I couldn't see it or trace it. If it wasn't for him, I truly don't know where I would be.

I would have never been able to get through any of my personal struggles if it wasn't for my strong foundation in Christ. All of my growth and change was due to him. Build a relationship with God, first. Let him show you unconditional love and be the father or mother you need him to be to you. He will give you more than you could ever imagine.

People often complain about their lives and their situation but when you try to give them the answer, they don't receive it.

Why are you even going to complain to someone or ask for help if you're not going to be receptive of it? We look for answers in other things instead of turning to the one main source that will give you every answer you need. The Bible says that in 1 John 4:9 "This is how God showed his love to us: He sent his one and only son into the world so that we could have life through him." Many of you don't have kids. However stop and think. If you had a child - your only child, would you be willing to make that big of a sacrifice for anyone? I definitely know that I wouldn't. God loved you and me so much he was willing to make that big of a sacrifice for us. That's a lot of love. I don't know about you, but that's definitely the type of love I want to be thrown at me. He is definitely someone I would give a chance. If He would do that for me, I know He has my best interest at heart. and He has a plan for my life.

Even in your sin and your worldly flesh, God will still love you. He welcomes you with open arms and holds you close. He cleans you up and begins to make you over again. Make Him the center of your life and let everything else revolve around Him.

CHAPTER 2

The Dating Game

"Dating is give and take. If you only see it as "taking", you're not getting it." ~Henry Cloud

When God finally does send someone in your life, make sure you take it slow and not rush into anything. Get to know all about the person before you start using the words, boyfriend and girlfriend. It's very important to establish a friendship foundation. First, you will always have that to revert back to when things aren't going as good as you had hoped. Too many people meet someone and they date for a couple of weeks and then they are calling each other boyfriend and girlfriend. I made that mistake once in my life.

I met this guy and we started talking. We talked for about a month, he asked me to be his girlfriend and foolishly I accepted. Growing up, I wasn't the girl that had a lot of attention from boys, so I never had a lot of boyfriends. I was swept off my feet by all the compliments and attention this one boy gave me. I said yes to being his girlfriend. Later I realized that I didn't like some of his character traits. He and I didn't even establish a friendship, so I didn't get to know him as well as I should have. He wanted different things in life that I just didn't want.

I was raised in church, so who ever I dated needed to have a relationship with God and he did not. He wanted to stay at home and watch church on the TV, which I thought was absolutely insane. I battled with breaking up with him or staying around to see if he would change, until finally I decided to call it quits. Too many times, we give our boyfriend/girlfriend a husband or wife qualifier. If you're just dating and you start to notice red flags, honey, I say get out then. Why stick around for it to only get worse? If he was my husband then I would have sought counseling, or something that I thought would be productive; but he wasn't. He was some boy that gave me a lot of compliments, and I liked that part of it. So when it boils down to it, no, I'm not giving you a chance to see if you can learn to love God or want to do something better with your life. These are things that should already be figured out. I broke up with him literally a month after being his girlfriend. I knew God had better for me. He and I didn't add to each other. If I'm with someone I need them to add to my life and make me a better person and I them. That was a lesson learned. From now on, I won't ever rush into another relationship. It's not worth it. I would rather take the time to really get to know a person and be his friend. By doing it this way, I can find out his family history, his goals in life, and if what he wants matches with what I want. Then we can talk about becoming more than that after I know all of what I need to know.

Always pay attention to where and how you meet the person you are going to be dating. Everyone meets people in different places. I'm sure you never really gave it a lot of thought. Where you meet a person can tell you a lot about their character. If you go out to the club with your girls, and you see a man popping crazy bottles, dancing with a lot of girls and just acting a fool, nine times out of ten that's the one that's going to try and talk to you (especially if you looking good that night). You turn him down, the first time. A few weeks later you will see him in the same club doing the same thing. He comes up to you again, with the tired game he uses on every other girl ...and this time you fall for it. You start dating and then a few weeks or months into the relationship, you're mad because he's going to the club popping bottles and dancing with a lot of females. Your intuition is telling you he might be cheating and doing things that he shouldn't be doing, if he is pursuing you.

Someone might ask why are you mad? He showed you who he was already and you didn't see the red flags. It's very important to pay attention to the signs and your female intuition which is nothing but discernment from God. You turned him down for a reason, the first time. Don't get side tracked by his persistence, that you forget to pay attention to the important stuff. How coincidental is it that you see the exact same man, in the exact same club, doing the exact same thing? You didn't give this man your number the first time. So it's not like you could tell him you were going to be there. The thought should have popped up that this is something he does every weekend or very often. You should have run then. Instead you thought he was being cute and persistent, so you started talking to him. You think because he is with you, all of a sudden, you can make him change and be home with you on the days he would normally be out at the club? Sorry, Boo, it's not going to happen. He is going to do him, regardless if you like it or not. I won't ever say never, but the chances of you being able to change a man are very slim. He is a man and set in his ways. Women by nature are nurturers and we want to fix everything, Its in our genes.. We will take on any challenge. Women can carry a lot. We are strong in our own right. So often times we will get with a man and see his potential! And then assume we can be the one to fix him. I hate to tell you that is a lie. First off, he's a grown man, not your son. Secondly, how do you know he is ready to change? One thing I do know, is when a man is ready for something else, he will hang up that player's card and he goes after what it is he wants. Also, men typically don't take well to a woman trying to change them because it makes them feel as though they aren't good enough how they are. You may have invested time into something that isn't going to work all because, you didn't pay attention to the obvious signs.

If you work at the mall and every two weeks or so, you see the same guy coming in shopping up all of his money, he is careless with his money. We all know every two weeks is payday and if the first thing he does is come in and shop, then he isn't going to really value money. Yes, we all deserve a treat if we have worked hard for our checks. But let's be smart with our money. If you start dating someone like this and the relationship progresses to marriage, how is he going to be with your joint account? Every time the new pair of Jordan's comes out, he may go and buy some for him and the kids. I plan to give my kids everything I didn't have growing up, but by no means will all of my money go to materialistic things. As women we tend to take these things lightly. Let's be honest, no one wants a man that can't dress and that doesn't have a nice pair of shoes. Eventually his little paycheck is going to turn into an even bigger one. What if he starts making $300,000 a year? That's even more money, which frees him to buy even bigger and more expensive things. You don't want to have to deal with the burden of a husband's bad spending problem. Just make sure who you are getting yourself involved with is someone who is responsible from the beginning. I watched the fabulous life of Kim and Kanye, the other day. The guy said that Kanye had seven cars, one for each day of the week. I laughed because we all know that Kanye is wealthy, but 7 cars really? That's a bit much. I understand him being able to afford it, but just because you can afford something, doesn't mean you should buy it. I think 3 or 4 cars would do him justice. Half the time he is on a plane or jet anyway. This is what we are not trying to become. I want all of you to become wealthy and successful, able to go out and buy whatever you want. But I also want you to be smart and realistic with your money. The Bible teaches us to be good stewards over our money. It saves you in the end. It will also save your relationship from financial trouble.. As an African American woman, I tend to notice that some of our people are so careless with money. We don't invest. We don't by stocks. We don't save. We live paycheck to paycheck working for the man and still having holes in our pockets.

One day, I asked my mom why was I working. I felt like I never have any money anyways. I might as well not work. We like to look good, at all times, have the newest outfits on, and the longest weaves. We walk by so many wealthy people every day. But you wouldn't know it by the way that they are dressed. Smart wealthy people have stocks, investments and all this other stuff. Their money makes money while they are sleeping. They don't need to wear $500 shoes all the time. Their bank account speaks for itself. The only way people in our world will start to look at us differently is if we've put some money away. We can yell all day "Black lives matter", but they won't matter if we as black people don't learn the value of a dollar. We need to come together and figure out how to band together and use our money to change the world. We could open youth centers to help get these young men off the streets. We could open schools, gas stations, etc. to offer job opportunities. But you can't change the world if all you are concerned with is when is Jordan making a new pair of shoes. Please note, I am not knocking people who do dress well and spend money on shoes because I also enjoy a little retail therapy. What I am saying is that it can't be your only focus and your main drive.

Make sure you also pay attention to how a man treats the important women in his life: his mom, grandmother, sister, daughter, aunts, etc. A man's first teacher is his mother and if he doesn't respect her what makes you think he will respect you? His mother plays the same role in his life that a father plays in yours. She teaches him how to love and treat a woman the correct way. She teaches him to avoid having several girls, but to find a nice girl and settle down. If he doesn't get the proper foundation from his mother, he won't treat you as you deserve, because he probably doesn't know how. Whether it is because his mom wasn't around to show him how to love and respect a woman or he just simply doesn't care and appreciate a woman, you want no parts of it. It will only end up bad for you and hurting you in the end. If he won't take care of her or give her the world he isn't going to take care of you or give you the world. The most common mistake women make is thinking they are that one that can make him treat her differently. We say things like "Ain't nobody gone hold him down like me so I know he gone do me right. Or he knows he's got a good thing in me and he don't want to lose me." While you think you are the girl that's gone make him want to treat you better, he may be talking to the next girl. If a man doesn't respect the woman that labored with him and gave birth to him, you're no exception. His mother raised him, stayed up with him at night, and was there for him when things were rough. You haven't even done half of what his mother has done for him.

What you have to watch out for is the man that will tell you he has a good relationship with his mother just to be with you. In reality he doesn't care 2 beans about her. This guy will talk a good game, but when he is around his mother you can tell he doesn't really care about her as he should. When you're around he'll kiss her on the cheek and greet her, but as soon as she asks for something, he really doesn't want to do it. He'll be slow to move, eventually he'll get to it because you're there. if you weren't there, he wouldn't have done it. Around Mother's Day, he'll spend all his money on himself and get his mother 1 rose or something cheap. Mother's Day shouldn't be about materialistic things but that's what society has made it. So if you have some money to buy your mom a nice gift, why wouldn't you? This man is selfish and only thinks about him. he will be the same way in his relationship with you and you should rethink wanting to be with that guy.

What you would hope to see is a man that loves and cherishes his mother. He calls her all the time to make sure she is ok, and doesn't need anything. He pulls her chair out for her, opens doors for her, and makes sure she has everything she needs. When he is around she knows she is safe and that he has her best interest at heart. He will go to war for his mother because he knows no one in his life can compare. His mother is his first love and she gave him life He is forever grateful and he will show her every day. I know it may sound corny but this is the man that will love you past life. Yea, he might come with a few bad bruises, but everyone has flaws. He will treat and love you like he loves his mother. He knows you two are the most important women in his life and he won't do anything to jeopardize that because it's too special.

You want to make sure that the person you date is on your level in all possible aspects. That means mentally, spiritually, emotionally and even sometimes physically. I say sometimes physically because, it shouldn't be all about looks. We have to be able to see past the looks of a person and see the heart of the person. Everyone has a particular type of guy that just turns them on, but what if in reality your Mr. Right looks nothing like that? Let's say you like a man that is light-skinned, tall, has dimples, a 6-pack, and nice teeth. You meet someone that meets all your physical expectations, but they can't meet you mental needs, or your spiritual needs. Maybe this guy looks good, but he doesn't treat you as well as you'd like, and he thinks you are the lucky one in the relationship, instead of you both are lucky to be with each other. He doesn't really want a commitment because he wants to test the grass and see if it really is greener on the other side, first. On the other hand, you have the guy that meets all your other expectations, but he has a chipped tooth, he isn't as tall as you'd like. He's dark skinned and he really isn't what you like physically. But, he makes you feel like a queen. He shows you all the love and affection he has to give to you. He takes you to nice places and stimulates your mind with conversation. He makes you feel like doing better with your life, because he challenges you to do better. What do you do? I hope everyone's answer would be to go with the guy that meets all of your other needs and not necessarily what you wanted physically. I had to learn this through talking to guys who I thought were so sexy but they were the ones that weren't good to me. I used to have a specific type which I would say was light-skinned guys. I said I would never date a dark-skinned guy unless it was Jimmy Butler (which was totally immature on my part). True love has no color so if you're looking for someone that will treat you like a queen and love you the way God intended, you have to get rid of the color barrier. We say what we will never date without even trying it first. You don't know you don't like carrots until you've actually tried carrots before. Now that I am older, I don't have a type. I don't want someone that is just totally not fit and all out of shape, but if a nice healthy (meaning kind of chubby) guy comes around I will talk to him because….big boys need love, too! It's all about what makes you happy as a person; you can't really care and think about what other people are going to say about you. I have learned over the years, people will talk about you and make you feel a certain way only because they want what you have. They will cause you to break up with your boyfriend because they will tell you, that you can do better. He isn't on your level. But as quick as you break up with him, they trying to get his number from him. You have to watch people. Every person in your life doesn't have your best interest at heart. You have to know the ones who do. At the end of the day, make sure you are happy and that's all that matters.

Sometimes while dating we can get so caught up in the fact that we are dating, that we simply forget to find out the important things about the other person. It's very important to find out what you need to know upfront because if you don't if you should find points of disagreement, it might be too difficult to leave, because by then your emotions are involved.

The most important thing I think is to find out their religious background if you're a religious person. You don't EVER want to date someone who doesn't have the same beliefs as you because, it will make things so complicated. Let's say you are a Christian and believe in Jesus Christ and the guy you're dating is Muslim and only believes in God and not in Jesus Christ. How would you make this work? The Bible says that God is a jealous God so are you going to compromise your faith for the sake of a boy? Hopefully not because it's absolutely not worth it. Religious differences are one of the biggest reasons couples breakup. Instead of waiting till God sends them the right person, they will sacrifice their religion for the sake of being with someone. God will never have our significant other be someone of a different faith. What would be the reason in that? It wouldn't make any sense at all! You guys will never see eye to eye. To some this might not seem like a big deal. As Christians, we try to persuade as many people to come to Christianity as we can, because we believe so strongly in it. Just like you have a strong belief about your faith, the other person might about their faith, as well. How can you persuade a Muslim to come to Christianity? If at the same time they are trying to persuade you to become Muslim? It will be a constant clash of the two and you will begin to bicker about it until one of you realizes it just isn't going to work. Although you call it quits, you're more likely to go back to that person because your emotions are tied to them. It is a difficult thing to leave someone after that.

What if you guys actually decided to both make it work knowing the different beliefs you have? Let's say you date avoiding all religious conversation, and then get married. When the children come you won't be able to avoid all the religious conversation. You are going to want your children to be raised as Christians and he, Muslim. The situation is way worse at this point because children are involved. You don't want your kids to see you arguing but it's beginning to be frustrating because neither of you are giving in. Who wins? Neither of you will win because a child can't be brought up in 2 faiths. It's either you believe Jesus Christ is your Lord and Savior and died on the cross for you or you don't. Don't let wanting to date make you a compromiser.

What if Jesus would have compromised your sins on the cross and said, "Well later on in life she's going to pick this boy over me so let me not die for her." You wouldn't have half the life you have now. He made a sacrifice for us, why can't we do the same for him? Often times we think God is ruining the fun or doesn't want us to be happy. I laugh at that because, he is looking down at us thinking the same thing, "Do you not want to be happy?" God doesn't want to take away the fun he wants you to have fun but in the right way. God does not want us to date someone who doesn't believe in Christ because he is trying to save your feelings. When bad things happen we ask God why? How could he let this happen to you? But he tells us how to prevent those things from happening. Often, we choose not to listen to him. We think we know better or that we have a short cut. So if you don't listen to the warning then all God can do is allow you to cry on his shoulder when the bad thing happens; because it definitely will.

We have to make sure that who we are dating is someone that we can bring home to mom and dad. We have to secure ourselves as a woman and make sure that this person is going to treat us with respect and love and cherish the relationship. We also have to make sure that before we fall in love, that we choose someone who will be successful and able to take care of his family. Ladies, this is where the backlash comes in from society.

The term "gold-digger" is one that really annoys me. I wish that it would disappear from our vocabulary. As a woman, you want to make sure that the guy you are dating is financially stable, or has a plan to get there and because of this you are titled as a gold-digger. I think it's the most absurd thing in the world. You have to make sure you are protected and taken care of because, if you don't, no one else will. Yes, you can be an independent woman and have your own money. You shouldn't need for him to do anything for you financially because you have your own. But, there ain't nothing wrong with wanting a man with some money. What woman wants to have to play the male role in her relationship? If you guys go out to a nice restaurant and the check comes he looks at you, after he knows he just ate a whole steak meal. The man in a relationship should be the provider and he should be paying for the dates until you guys reach a certain level in your relationship. Then I think it's absolutely ok for the woman to treat the man, but that's something that is earned not given right off the bat. I haven't had any experience in a guy not wanting to pay for the meal but I'm sure some of you have. It's pathetic. If a man wants to take you out he needs to know that he will be paying the bill. If you are dating someone with no money or aspirations in life, how is he going to pay the bill? You both will be in the kitchen at Red Lobster busting suds. You want to make sure you are getting yourself involved with someone who is on your same level. He has the same drive and zeal for life as you do. He wants to make something of himself, as you do. He is trying to be better than the world makes him out to be. When you meet him and he asks you out, make sure you ask him about his goals in life. Find out if he has a plan to get where he is trying to go. By asking all of these questions you will find out straight from the horse's mouth exactly what you need to know. A man can wish and have all the dreams in the world, but if he wants to date me I'm going to need him to have some of them dreams In the works already. If society wants to call you a gold-digger for making sure that your time isn't being wasted, then by all means let them feel free. No woman wants to be with a man that won't push himself to do better or that is just comfortable with their lives and where they are; which isn't really anywhere to begin with.

Men sometimes need to be pushed and if you can be that woman to give that man that push, then do so. Society has pushed our African American men to feel as though they will never be anything in life. The standard for them is set so low that sometimes they feel like what's the point in even trying if I'm going to face so much adversity. But that's actually the time for them to do what they need to do to be able to prove the world wrong and make a difference. I'm not telling you if you meet someone and he doesn't make or have six figures in the bank to leave him. That would be absolutely insane but you want to make sure that he has a plan to better his life. If he does have a plan then by all means discuss it with him and see if there are parts where you can help. It might mean just being his motivator and encourager or actually putting in time to help him develop his plan. Make sure you aren't getting hyped over his potential to be a good successful man. Women tend to work off of the potential In a man. We see what they can become instead of what they really are. All men have a lot of potential but you want to make sure you see some of that potential flourish into reality while you guys are together. If not, then you are going to get stuck with false hope and false potential. Women have to learn how to keep their eyes open and on the goal and not look further ahead then what they see; because sometimes that can be a stumbling block.

For example if I met someone that wants to play pro basketball. He obviously isn't going to have 6 figures in the bank just yet but if I like him I will stick around to see where this goes. Now if I stick around and try to help him reach his goal of playing pro ball, and every time I call him he's at home on the couch playing video games...I'm going to have a problem with that. Or If I encourage him to go to the gym to do his conditioning or whatever he needs to do to make the team, and he's always too tired or got something else to do.....I'm going to have a problem with that. I will try and sit down and talk to him about his position and what schools would be best at helping him develop that position more. I will also let him know he really isn't giving me anything to work with. I'm trying to be the good supportive girlfriend but He isn't trying hard enough to get to the Pro's. He can't want to play ball and then when it comes to doing the things he needs to do he doesn't ever do any of them, what sense does that make? I can only encourage him for so long before I start to question if this is something he really wants to do. I can't want it more than he does, because it's not my dream. At this point, I would have a conversation with him and let him know the things

I'm noticing and that he has to do better or I am going to leave him. If after a few weeks, he is still sitting on that same couch with that same video game, I'm going to keep good on my promise and leave. Why would I waste my time? He obviously has a goal but isn't ready to reach it yet. He isn't prepared to do the things it takes to get him to where he is trying to go. This is a good example of false potential. He could be one of the best basketball players in the world but how will I ever know if he doesn't test the skill out every now and then to enhance it.

He needs time to find himself and figure out his life. Let's face it every day isn't going to be all good; everyone has good and bad days. It will be the same in a relationship, but to sit around and stay with someone who can't even get off their buts to make a better life for themselves is something that shouldn't be tolerated.

What good is it doing you to stick with a man like that? If he won't even do it for himself, you most certainly can't force him to do it for you. If it's your boyfriend or someone your dating and you like them a lot, you should absolutely support him if their going through something very rough and traumatic. I'm not saying to leave them if they fall on hard times because the way the economy is, that can happen to anybody at any given time. You can support them and encourage them to get up and do better or even go into business for themselves, but don't let him sit in his pity and not go looking for another job or just get comfortable with not working. The Bible says, if a man doesn't work, he doesn't eat. And in Genesis, the Lord coursed Adam and told him that from now on his work would cause him turmoil and sweat in his brow... meaning that he would have to work hard in this world to survive because he ate from the serpent as Eve did. The point I'm trying to make is nothing comes easy and for our men unfortunately working hard is something they inherited from Adam in the bible.

Now, some men when you meet them, like I said, they won't have it all together. But if they take the relationship seriously, they will begin to try and figure it out. He knows he has a good thing in his girl and he wants to be with her for a long time. Using the same example from earlier; if this man that knows he doesn't have it all together, but wants to figure it out, he will take completely different steps than the other guy. His path will be dedicated to achieving his goals for the bettering of his relationship. He will get up early in the morning and hit the gym to do his training. He will change his diet to eat the things he needs to eat to build muscle and strength. He'll practice his skill to make sure it's up to par with everyone else or even better. He shows you great effort and makes you feel like he'll give you the world with his determination and hard work. Sure, he will get tired and face adversity because everyone does when they are trying to reach a goal. But the difference is, he won't fold under the pressure because he knows he has a job and that is to be the man in his family. Even when you feel tired and question if it is ever going to happen, he won't let you lose your faith in him. To a man, it's very important that he shows his lady that he can be the man that she needs him to be. It's also important that she never stops believing in him. His masculinity is everything to him. He will do everything not to compromise that in any way with her. So proving he has what it takes to take care of his family is his way of not compromising that. This is the kind of man you want.

In addition to finding out all you need to know, make sure you set your expectations in the beginning. You don't want to beat around the bush with this because it's a rather important step. It's very important for the man to know what kind of woman he is dealing with and what he can and can't do with you. I find that women normally wait until they feel they know the person better to lay down the dos and the don'ts. I think that's backwards. In the beginning there aren't really any emotions attached. You can tell him what you expect and he can stay if he thinks he can meet/exceed those expectations, or he can leave because he knows he can't meet those expectations. If he stays, great. However, if he leaves then it's not like you're going to be crying for days and listening to sad love songs because you really didn't know him like that to begin with. Men try and act like they hate women that set rules and have boundaries but at the end of the day they have to respect it. If you want your man to be faithful, honest, and loyal make sure you explain what that looks like to you. That's important because he may have a different picture in his head. Although it seems self-explanatory, break it down so he understands and won't be able to come back and say he didn't know what you meant. This is your life and you have to take control of it. Let him play your game and you call the shots because, if he wants to date you he has to know that you aren't going to settle for less than what you deserve. I heard someone once use the analogy than men were like houses and women were like cars, and someone asked Kim Kardashian why she didn't have any tattoos and she responded and said because you wouldn't put a bumper sticker on a Bentley would you? So therefore I'm not putting any ink on my body. She referred to herself as a Bentley, which is a very expensive and beautiful car. I think a lot of us only view ourselves as Honda Civics and that's no shade to people that have and make Honda Civics. However, if given the choice of a free Honda or a free Bentley you would take the Bentley because it's detailed, expensive and it looks nicer. Ladies, value yourself and it will get you a long way. Having self-respect and confidence is the sexiest thing a woman can wear. No real man wants a woman who will allow anything. If she allows him to do anything then she's allowed others to do anything as well. Beyoncé said that girls run the world and I think its fine time that we step into that role and be the bosses I know we can be.

In a relationship, it's very important that the woman doesn't lose her own identity. Women tend to sometimes take the backseat for a man. Especially if they're older because they're looking for a husband not a boyfriend. If you're 16 or 17 years old you don't have to worry about this because, you are just starting to date and you really aren't thinking about marriage just yet. When you reach the age of 20+, your mindset changes, and you think about your future. This includes the type of man you want and having a family. Men often times want a woman that will be a stay at home wife, take care of the kids, cook, and clean. They believe men should be the bread winners and the woman should hold down the fort. For some couples, this works, the women don't mind staying at home taking care of the kids. But those women may eventually start to feel like they are behind their spouses and not standing beside them as they should be. I think to the man, if his lady is working and making her own money he feels threatened by that. This is because he knows she really doesn't need him for anything financially. Men like the power of knowing that they are needed by their ladies, which is why some of them don't want their ladies to work. On Real Housewives Of Atlanta, Porsha Williams was married to Kordell Stewart and he was the man that didn't want her to work. He wanted her to stay at home and work and take care of his son, which was her stepson. She agreed and was fine taking care of the child and staying at home. She had what seemed to be the perfect life. She had designer bags, clothes, shoes and a big house. Later on in the season she realized she was ready to start trying for kids again but she wanted to be a working mother now. Kordell didn't agree. He didn't want her to have her own identity he wanted to be the only bread winner in the family. They couldn't work out their differences and they divorced later in the show.

Yes, women should take care of their families and make sure the uphold of the house is ok. But who says that's all we're supposed to do? We don't want to feel like our only jobs are cooking, cleaning, and taking care of kids. We can do that and so much more. We have goals and things that we want to accomplish in life as well. So why should we diminish our goals for the sake of some man's ego? I admired Porsha taking a stand and saying she can have both a family and a career. When her husband wanted to compromise that she signed those divorce papers and got herself out of that situation. People might have thought she was crazy because, let's be honest, she had the ideal life. It was what we all are working towards. She sacrificed it all for the sake of being a business woman and at the end of the day we have to respect that because it took guts. Men need to realize we don't want to diminish their ego as men but we want to build our ego as women. We don't want to always ride in the backseat. Sometimes we want to drive and show that we are not just the wives or girlfriends of some successful man. We are successful in our own rights as well. We don't want to get so caught up in being a good wife and mother that we lose our individuality.

I love to see women with successful husbands like Michelle Obama, Beyoncé, and Erica Campbell take a stand and make their own money. They are determined to leave a legacy behind and not just live off of their husbands. This is encouraging to me because they made a choice to do better. How many of us given a choice to have their rich and successful husband take care of them, would choose to go to work instead? Not many of us would, but it takes a strong woman to want to be the different one and not take the easy route out.

Be a strong woman and make your own decisions about your life. Get up and make a name for yourself. Don't be comfortable and settle for anything. If your husband is successful let him live in his success and make sure you find yours as well and live in that. Don't take away from him being the man but definitely walk beside him and not behind him. It should be a democracy and not a dictatorship. However, the Bible destined for the man to lead the household and be the leader of his family. I whole heartedly believe in this. When the time comes I will have no problem submitting to my husband because that's order. To become a good leader we must learn to follow first. However, if a man is going to lead me I'm going to need him to know where he is going. I need him to have plans for our family. What's the plan for our children? How are we going to build our future? How are we going to help advance the kingdom of God together? I need to know that he has been before God and that he has asked God for wisdom and direction on leading this family. If we have a conversation and can't come to an agreement I want him to tell me that we need to pray and seek God first and then go from there. I want a husband that will follow Christ as we follow him.

Now women in relationships can do some stupid things that can make men not want to be with us as well. We have to learn to be wise in our actions and how we handle them as men. Women are very smart and we pay close attention to things that men don't think we pay close attention to. We pay attention to things that are triggers to the man. If we then get into an argument then we have something to say that will hurt the man. This is a young tactic I think younger couples use this because it's all about getting you before you get me. Some women have been wounded by different men so much to the point that they carry the baggage from the last guy into the relationship with the new guy. If your last guy cheated on you, you're so busy trying to make sure the new guy doesn't cheat that you're actually pushing him away or even worse, towards another woman. You're so paranoid and insecure that every time he leaves you're worrying sick about where he is, who he is with, and if he is being faithful to you. When he comes home you're accusing him of cheating, asking him what's the other woman's name and he doesn't have a clue what you're talking about. You keep trying to make him the last guy and you keep digging for trouble, if you dig a hole deep enough, you're going to find what you are looking for. If you keep accusing him of cheating sooner or later he will go and actually cheat on you. You continuing to accuse him doesn't make it right but at the same time it's like ok you wanted to keep accusing me of doing something let me go and do it then. Once he finally does cheat on you then you screaming I knew you were like whoever your last boyfriend was that cheated on you. We have to make sure that we are ready to be in a relationship with someone and that we are emotionally ready. That man could have been a good man but she didn't get the chance to experience that because her emotions were still in her last relationship. She made him out to be what the last man was before he got the chance to prove himself different. This is a common mistake I see on a day to day basis and it pains me because, I feel like women have passed up some good men because they couldn't put the past in the past and start fresh. Make sure that you are done with your first situation before you get into another one.

    Something else women do that I think we need to get out of

the habit of doing is, choosing the wrong guy. I say choosing because ultimately it's your decision who you end up being in a serious relationship with. You can date however many people and out of the bunch you will choose who you think suits you better, most of the time you are way off in the situation. If you are dating two guys and one guy is nice, caring, and giving you all of what you want that's the one we don't want. He's the guy that will call you to make sure you had a good day, text you and let you know he is thinking of you, and will give you all of him. The other guy is rude, self-centered, and doesn't make you feel like you're special to him. He may text you every now and then and when he does it's a simple "hey." Unfortunately, he will be the one that we go after and try and make our 'boo thang'. You can clearly tell he doesn't care about you as well as your other friend does but you don't care all you see is a challenge. The challenge of being able to make him see how good you are, or that he would have fun with you is what women like. But in reality it's the most foolish thing because if someone doesn't really want to be with you why would you want to make them want to be with you? Especially when you have someone else showing full interest in you. The reason is because you think that you can test the water and just have the nicer guy hanging by strings and just waiting for you to come around, and realize he is the better guy for you, or because your self-esteem is so low that you actually don't believe you deserve better. News flash, boo, no man is going to do that. The nice one is going to leave and find a girl that really values him and his personality. Now you have just lost out on a really nice guy for a foolish guy who doesn't want you obviously. You still are trying to make him see you by texting him all the time, and calling him all the time. You're checking Facebook, Instagram, Twitter, and Snapchat to see what he's posting about. That's just giving way too much energy to someone who doesn't deserve it. Then we screaming and crying that there aren't any good men in the world, but there are. We just don't pay them any attention until it's too late. Then we mad at the next girl that got the good guy you didn't want until it was too late. It's not her fault she realized what you didn't. Another thing ladies do is choose the thug over the smart guy because they think he is more fun and fulfilling. When did dating a smart guy become lame? Since when did everybody want to date a clown? There's is nothing wrong with wanting a man to be able to protect you if you're in danger because that's sexy. But some girls want the for real dangerous life, someone who will pack on 3 guns just to walk down the street. They having a gang fight every two days, and he getting shot at and cut up. What girl wants to live this life with someone that's not even their husband? I wouldn't even want to live that life with my husband so especially not someone I'm just dating. It's stupid to want to put your life in danger for a man who you might not even be with 3 months from now. He gets into with some girls so now you got to go and fight for him and you getting your hair pulled out and getting black eyes; it's too much.

Those are the girls we call ride or die chicks, but it's the stupid chick because you don't want to be that type of girl. Girls try and live up to this standard and for what? One; you're not a chick, you are a young lady. Two; why would you support a man in doing something foolish? He tells you he thinking about going and getting a couple of guns to go and shoot up Lil' Ray Ray crib, and you tell him you know where he can get the gun for a good price and that you will accompany him there. That's foolish to me, just because he wants to put himself in danger doesn't mean you should. As I researched the term "Ride or Die chick," I found a disturbing song by LOX feat. Timberland and EVE. The song is called "Ryde or die Bitch". It talks about what the "Ryde or die Bitch" is to them basically. Here are a few of the lyrics...

"Mom's babysitting, ain't seen her in a week. I'm a bad influence to parents that hate the Sheek. I need a ryde or die bitch that'll take this coke out of town and come back and breakdown when I'm broke." WHAT? This song was created in 1999 and was on the Album titled "We Are The Streets." This song was the most successful song off the entire album peaking at #73 on Billboard 100, #27 on hot R&B/Hip-hop songs, and #22 on the hot rap singles. Apparently, people were feeling this song and the message it had to send out. This particular verse talks about a woman who has children and leaves them with her mother to go and do 'God knows what' with this man. He wants a woman that will carry drugs for him and take it to its proper destination. Listening to this song, I was disgusted because who wants that life for themselves? Running around town, taking stuff here and there for some man that's probably got 4 other girls doing the same thing. It makes me angry at the women who do stoop down to these levels. In the song EVE was talking about how she drive "Cadillac trucks with her girls in the back" and her "Prada suits fit cause her ass is fat." How you getting them Prada suits and them Cadillac trucks? Women want to live this fancy lavish lifestyle but don't want to put in the work to get there. If you got up and stopped trying to be a ride or die chick, you could go to school, get an education, and make your own money. Then you can keep driving your Cadi and wearing your Prada suits but feel good about it because, you worked for it. Not delivering some drugs over here, and holding his gun in your house for him. As a thank you or to keep you quiet he gives you a couple stacks. Another way women earn the title ride or die chick is by staying with their man, even if he continuously cheats. I hate when I hear celebrity males say it comes with the territory or she knows "wassup" when I'm on the road. They use these words as if it makes it ok for them to go and do what they do. If you can't keep your private in your pants then I'm sorry you don't need to go on the road or you need to be single. I'm not about to let a man walk all over me as these girls do for the sake of keeping a happy home, or keeping the lifestyle that I'm used to living. Baby, bye. I'll give it all up and start all over again, because my heart is no doormat. I'm not about to let a man cheat on me multiple times, and I continue to come back to him. Honestly, I would maybe give him one good time to mess up with cheating. I would try and figure out why he felt the need to cheat and was it something I did or didn't do. We would fix it and move on. But to try and play me three, four, and five times is absolutely not going to happen. I'm sorry I will not be that ride or die chick.

The urban definition of a ride or die chick is "a chick that ain't afraid to be down with her man. She'll do anything for her man he needs her to." Further down some synonyms for the term are Gutta Bitch and Bottom Bitch. These are terms that some men refer to women, as if we are always down for the ride or willing to do anything for them. If a female calls a woman a Bitch then she gets mad and is ready to fight but if her boyfriend calls her a Gutta Bitch then it's ok, because it's like an accolade to her. That's called having a double standard. If one person can't do it then it shouldn't be ok for anyone to call you that. What has happened to our self-esteem as women that we even aspire to be a ride or die chick? A real man doesn't want that. He wants a woman that's going to stand by his side and tell him when he is about to make a mistake, or tell him I don't think you should do that. He wants a woman that will help him build his empire. I don't think you can do that if you trying to be a ride or die chick, because one day you gone have to take the fall for it all. Who cares what people will say or if he threatens to leave for the girl that will do everything? Chuck up them deuces and keep it moving because your future is too bright to lose it all over some fool that isn't worth it. If anything, be the ride or die chick that will challenge him to do better, and make him think twice before doing something that is dangerous. No woman should want a man that wants her to even be a part of his foolishness because what does that say about him? And to be completely honest, it's just a matter of time before he starts being tough with you, and hitting you. That's eventually all that path leads to and that's something you don't want to have to deal with. Choose wisely who you spend your time with and make sure it's someone with a nice head on his shoulders.

Those of you who may be involved with someone who you can't get over, or think you will have feelings for them forever. Let me be the first to tell you that you definitely can get out of that situation. You don't need to stay with someone who is disrespectful and not treating you like you deserve to be treated. Every girl deserves someone who will treat her like a queen and know that she is the best thing to ever happen to him. We, as ladies, have to know this first because; guys are not stupid at all. They know the girls who they can catch with a few clever lines from their tired game. You don't want to be that girl because she is the one who is the side chick and that he only takes out at night or either early in the day. She gets the late night booty call/texts and my favorite excuse "Oh baby, my phone died. That's why I didn't get your call or text." Those girls who guys can play like that are the girls who don't think they are queens and they don't know their own self-worth. They normally don't know because they haven't been told that they are queens or that they are beautiful and that they are worth so much more.

There was this boy I liked so much when I was a little girl. I thought he was the cutest boy I had ever seen. We went to the same elementary school for 8 years and then we graduated and went to different high schools. I liked him all of that time because I still thought about him occasionally. When we were in school together I knew he liked me, too. But we never acted on it because we were just too young. I don't know what it was about this boy that I liked him so much; but it was something because I did. We ended up connecting again on Facebook and we started texting and talking on the phone working towards what I thought was a relationship. He obviously had other plans. To me, it felt forced like I was trying too hard; which I probably was because I had liked him for so long. So I decided to back off a little because I didn't want to seem so desperate and obvious. When I backed a off a little, he completely stopped talking to me, no more phone calls/texts. All communication was cut off on his end. I did not understand what happened or what I did wrong. Of course my feelings were hurt, because I thought that this was finally our time to be together. I couldn't understand why he was so mad, just because I wouldn't force myself on him. He didn't want to go out he just wanted to talk on the phone, at night time. I knew I deserved better. It was obvious that he might not be for me, because all I did was pull back a little and he stopped talking to me. Then hit me. He stopped talking to me because I was his side chick. He never really cared as much as I did. He only wanted to pump my head up to see how long he could keep me thinking we were going to be boyfriend and girlfriend. We stopped talking for a while.

Then one day he decided to message me on Facebook and talk to me. At first, I played it cool and as if I didn't care. I secretly did care because even after all that, I still liked him. Stupidly, I started talking to him again. Everything was going good and then it got too good to be true. We had an argument and we both said some rude things to each other and just like that again we weren't speaking. I called and texted him. Either I didn't get a reply or if I did, it was very dry and rude. Then one day I got on Facebook and saw he had uploaded pictures of him and his new girlfriend. Now mind you we had only stopped talking like a week before. So once again, my feelings were hurt, but this time much worse. The new girl had been around. He had been talking to this girl and had me on the side again. I was mad at myself because I knew I shouldn't have been talking to him in the first place. I felt stupid and like a loser. I couldn't believe I allowed him to do this to me, again. Then on top of that, his new girl looked exactly like me and had the same name as me. At this point, I was too done. "Like you really gone try and play me and with a knock off version of myself". In the famous voice of my favorite star, Tamar Braxton, "You gone play with this puppy?"

I felt so disrespected and couldn't believe he had done that to me and he knew how much I liked him. On the opposing end, I should have known that he would do that to me again because he did it the first time. But thanks to him, I learned how not to let a man treat me. It wasn't a good feeling, like I was always competing against someone else. If anything he should have been competing for me, not the other way around. That was the last straw for me with him because I didn't like getting my feelings hurt. The day I realized this, was another turning point in my life because it made me stronger. It made me have to deal with and figure out what it was that made me crazy about this boy and pretty much burn all of those feelings. There was a time I thought that I would like him forever and if he contacted me I would be down for the ride. But not anymore, he had the vulnerable Ebony who was just now figuring out who she was. She didn't really value herself because of self-esteem issues and other personal things. But I want young girls to know I don't care what you look like or where you come from; NEVER let a man or boy treat you like his second choice. You are worth so much more than that and you have to stand up for yourself and say what you will and will not tolerate in a relationship. Never tolerate being cheated on, lied to, and physically or mentally abused. Don't ever feel as though you can't leave because that's the best you can do. You are a strong, beautiful woman and you can have any man you want. So why settle for the low life? Don't cheat yourself out of something great for something late. Treat yourself as though you are the prize. Make them play your game to win you. The name of my game is Ebony and the winner will be whoever passes each level and whoever is the last one standing.

Also, in dating and having a relationship with someone, you have to be ready to give, sacrifice and compromise. Now, when I say compromise I don't mean compromise your goals, morals, or faith. I mean compromise like not arguing about stupid things such as where the next date will be, or if he can go hang out with his guys. I know some girls feel that since they are the girls in the relationship that they should call all the shots. But remember you're not in a relationship with yourself. There is another person with their own likes and dislikes. It can't be all about you and you getting what you want all time. A relationship is about give and take. You give a little and he gives a little to make it work. One person shouldn't be giving more than the next because it's not fair. If you are dedicated to the relationship then that means not getting your way sometimes. He gets to do things he likes as well. Men don't like to be with us all day long. Yes, I do believe that they should want to see us and spend time with us but to a degree. I think the relationship would get boring if you were in each other's faces all day long. There wouldn't be any time to miss each other. The saying, 'absence makes the heart grow fonder' is actually very true. It's in the time apart that you get to see where your relationship really is. When you're not together and he doesn't run across your mind, then you might not like him like that. If you realize you miss him more than you thought you would, and you keep thinking about him then you know he means something to you. It makes you see really if you should stick around or say deuces to him, especially if you have been together for a while. If it's been a short period of time then I would definitely say give it more time. We are the more attachment type, we like hugging, kissing, and holding hands because it's in our nature. But men don't feel like that all day long sometimes it's healthy for them to go and kick it with their friends. Just like time apart will help you to see where the guy stands in your life then it will help the guy to see where you stand with him. If you guys go a few days without seeing each other and you find yourself not thinking about him at all or he not thinking about you at all, then you guys should be worried because there is a disconnect. I remember dating guys, and if it was somebody that I was really feeling, if we weren't together, I would think about them all the time and he better had been thinking about me.

I think sometimes, women have gone through so much and because of the way that they were raised, it makes it hard for us to compromise; and give and not receive. It makes you feel like you are being walked over or taken advantage of, when in reality, you are just taking the steps it takes to be in a relationship. There is no way possible to have a relationship and you not have to give a little and compromise on some things. So if you aren't willing to do that, then how are you going to have relationships? And it's not only with a man. In any relationship you have, there will have to be sacrifices made because it takes two. This is why it is so important to be able to deal with the past hurts you have because they show up in other ways later on. In the Wounded Warriors conference, one of the workshops was on being able to deal with your soul. That's the thing that needs to be changed in order for you to really be able to move past those stumbling blocks. For example, if you were 15 years old and you witnessed your father always putting down and verbally abusing your mother, when you get older, you may struggle when the man tries to be the man in the relationship. What I mean is, if you guys are having a conversation and he is trying to get his point across to you, his voice might get elevated. Now to him it doesn't mean anything that his voice octave has changed because that's just how he gets his point across. But to you, when his octave raised you just saw him jump across the table and punch you in the throat and belittle you as a woman. Now, in your heart, you know that is something he would never do to you. But because you haven't dealt with the fear and the pain that you felt from your father abusing your mother, every time his voice raises that's the place you go to. Another example is if you grew up with a mom who would always give and give to her spouse and she never receives anything in return. That might make you angry watching your mom go through that. Her spouse isn't really appreciative of everything she does for him because he thinks that's what she is supposed to do. So some odd years later when you're in a relationship and the guy needs you to give more of yourself or do more to make him feel appreciated, you won't. In the back of your head, you're thinking "well you won't use me" or "I'm not your maid, do it yourself. if I do it, you wouldn't appreciate it anyway." You carry those weights with you all of these years and they start to show up in your own lives. Now you don't understand it, and you don't understand why him asking you for a little more time or to do a little more for him makes you so angry. Or if raising his voice signals to you that he is about to punch your brains out. It all reverts back to your childhood and the things you either personally went through or that you witnessed. The speaker of the workshop was saying that it's like an iceberg. As big as it is, people really only see about a good 10% of it. Nobody sees the other 90%. And that's exactly what we do with these childhood memories. She said we allow a person to see the 10% that looks good, we smile in their faces and we hug them tight and make them feel like we aren't going through anything. But deep down inside, the 90% is about to kill us because it's the sensitive area. She said it's the sensitive area that we don't want to touch or deal with because then that means some serious praying and warfare because you know how jacked up you really are. But once you allow God to touch that place and clean it out, then you will start to see a difference in how you react with people and your spouse. You won't take things so personally because you know it's not an attack on you. That's just the person's way of communicating.

CHAPTER 3

EMBRACING YOUR FLAWS

"Pretty hurts we shine the light on whatever's worse perfection is a disease of a nation pretty hurts pretty hurts pretty hurts we shine the light on whatever's worse try to fix something but you can't fix what you can't see it's the soul that needs a surgery" – Beyoncé

What do you consider to be beautiful? What do you think you need or don't need to have what is considered the look? As girls now a day it's very difficult to be comfortable with yourself if you don't have the proper foundation. We have beautiful people who we see all the time in magazines, videos, movies, and elsewhere such as Beyoncé, Tamar Braxton, and Ciara. The one thing they all have in common is they all sing, they all live lavish lives, and they are all light skinned. Now, I love them all and I'm sure you do as well but to what extent? Is your confidence so low that you wish you were them, wish you could be light skinned? Have you ever considered when you get older getting plastic surgery? I know I have and I know you have to. What makes us not love ourselves the way God intended for us to? The media and the entertainment industry play a nice role in this in my perspective. I feel like they are in control and have the power to judge what is pretty and what is not pretty. If you're like me you love looking at the magazines and looking at the latest fashion. If every time you pick up a magazine you see a light skin girl on the cover, and you don't look like that, it's going to strike something in you. It will make you feel like you don't have the look, which weighs on your self-esteem. You begin to question your own beauty. Is it good enough to be on the cover of Vogue magazine, can you be on the cover of any magazine with your dark skin? When I was a little girl this was my story. I hated being a dark skinned girl.

LIGHT SKIN VS DARK SKIN

When I was younger I had given all of my confidence to the media to determine my beauty. I never had a lot of confidence because I hated my skin color. There wasn't anyone around that could tell me that light skin wasn't prettier than dark skin. I had never been called ugly in my life because I wasn't light. Everyone around me would tell me how cute I was. But if it's not in your own heart, you absolutely won't believe them. I had my days where I did feel pretty and then there were those days where I felt so ugly.

I used to love singing when I was younger so of course my career choice was to be a singer. I listened to Beyoncé all of the time she was my role model. I felt like she was the epitome of a beautiful woman. Everyone wanted to either sing like Beyoncé or look like her. I knew I could sing so I wanted to look like her. I loved how she looked beautiful in everything. There was not a time we saw her that she didn't look fabulous. Beyoncé was on everything: bill boards, and magazines all the time. I wanted that life and that look for myself. I never went to extreme measures as far as doing anything to myself but I definitely had the thoughts. I didn't want to bleach my skin to get it lighter, but I know that for some people bleaching their skin would have been no problem. I remember watching the Tyra Banks show and she did an episode on this subject and the number of women that were affected by light skin vs. dark skin was actually sad. Women on the show arguing about what they go through and how hard they have it in the world because of their skin color. Not really realizing that they are fighting the same battle but just through different lenses. They all were fighting for the right to be themselves and live happily in their own skin.

Dark skinned women were arguing that lighter skinned black women have it way easier in the world than they do. Because they are of a darker skin, people tend to look at them as if they are dirty or don't meet some standard of beauty. There were even young girls on the show complaining about their skin colors and other things they hated about themselves. This is a real issue in the world and it affects women every day. No matter how much progress has been made there will still be some women who believe they are better because of their skin color. It really saddens me now because, I truly believe everyone is beautiful in their own way. How boring would the world be if we all looked the same? If we were all one shade and one size and one height? I think it would be boring because there's no uniqueness in the world. When different people come together and reproduce it makes a beautiful thing in the world.

My self-esteem was so low that I started to grow a dislike for people that were lighter than me. I never acted on my dislike as far as verbally saying something, and I could be right in front of someone lighter than me and act like nothing was wrong. But in the back of my head I was jealous of them because they had what was considered "the look". I used to live with a cousin, named Raveen. She and I could never get along when we were younger. At the time, I thought because we were cousins we were supposed to fight and have problems. We lived together and saw each other all the time. What else are we supposed to do? But that was not the case at all. Once I got older and was able to face my truth, I was able to admit that I was jealous of her look. She was lighter than me and I was so envious. I think the color barrier for me came from watching videos all the time, looking at magazine covers and not really seeing anybody that looked like me on them. I only saw white or light skinned girls, which caused me to think that was the hot thing to be and if you weren't, you were not beautiful. The media at the time were the ones to blame for this because they are the ones that dictate what's hot and what's not. If every time you pick something up and read it it's about someone who has lighter skin than you it raises the question; are you good enough? I think then the media did a bad job of showing a diverse group of women. They only catered to one specific group and left the girls with dark skin out of the equation. For the sake of dark skinned girls growing up feeling ugly and hating themselves, they should have made it more of a priority to bring in change and make things more equal. I understand that business is all about what sells, but sometimes you have to do things just strictly based on right and wrong. Who knows what seeing a dark skinned girl on the cover of a lucrative magazine could have done for a little black girl? She could have made the decision to live instead of committing suicide. She could have valued herself enough to not offer herself to the first boy that came along. People need to take into consideration that everything that they do has a cost and it could be at someone else's expense.

    Something else I even noticed is that the opposite sex had fallen into the cycle of doing the same thing. The men now would put down darker skinned women and make them feel like they weren't pretty. Using comments like "oh you're pretty for a dark skinned girl" or "in a dark alley all we can see are your eye balls." As a young girl, you know of course you want to be liked especially by the opposite sex because that's just how girls are. So to actually hear them say these evil things is heart breaking. It's not like we can argue against it because it seems to be proven true every time you look around at something. Now we have the media telling us darker skin isn't cute and now hearing it from boys and men. It weighs heavily on the mind because who wants to live in a world and feel beneath someone all the time. There was a point where I'm sure most dark skinned women, if up against a lighter black woman would feel she wouldn't get the job. I think the bosses would look at the two and racially profile them and assume that because one is lighter she is mixed with something. They'd assume she may be better or smarter at the job. When in actuality you can be getting the dumbest person in America and passing over the more qualified person all because of an assumption. What I want to make clear is that I'm not trying to bash on light skinned people, because some of my favorite people are lighter than me. But, back then, I wasn't able to think as clearly and more realistically like I do now. It doesn't do me any good to be angry at all light skinned people. All of them aren't arrogant or feel like they are better in any way. You have some light skinned people that will take a stand for you, such as the

Beyoncé's of the world. Beyoncé is one to encourage others to do whatever they want no matter what a person's skin color or race for that matter. She believes that we are all beautiful no matter how light or dark our skin is. Dark skinned girls have to learn to take what we have and own it. Make our dreams come true. We have so many inspiring people to look up to now in the world that we should be proud of them and be proud to be a dark skinned girl. Personally, I do feel like the media and society has gotten better at accepting darker skin and its beauty. We have magazine covers now, and we have movies that star women of darker skin. They fought and pressed to get what they have so that it would be a little easier for you and I. We should be so proud and appreciative for the talented actress Gabrielle Union, The musically talented Kelly Rowland, our beautiful first lady Michele Obama and the walking talent of Naomi Campbell. All of these women are dark skinned and beautiful in their own right. They don't let their skin color stop them from getting where they want to go, and this is what we have to learn to do.

Even before the media I think another thing that started this war was slavery. Back then for blacks, the job you had depended on how light or dark you were. If you were darker you got to work out in the field and in the hot sun. But if you were lighter then, you were given a bit of a pass and could work on the inside of the house, not in the hot sun. I think the masters assumed that the lighter skin possibly meant that one of the other masters could have slept with the woman and created a seed together which would be a lighter baby. This is why our black women look at each other defiantly and have their noses turned up as if they are better than someone else. This was something forced upon us in slavery we might have not been there actually in the field but because of that, we are still affected today. It makes me angry because I wish everyone could see the bigger picture and see that the color of your skin is the least of your worries. Women have so many other barriers to push through that the color of their skin should be at the very bottom.

    I never vocalized how I was feeling to anyone because I was embarrassed. I had been raised in church so I knew I was supposed to love myself, no matter what. But I couldn't shake how I was feeling so I was dealing with all of these emotions by myself. My mistake was in my silence. If I had been bold enough to open my mouth and express how I felt to someone I could have gotten help. Never be afraid to talk to someone about how you are feeling. Find a teacher, friend, parent, counselor, cousin, aunt anyone who you feel comfortable confiding in. Talking is the primary way to free yourself of anything you are feeling. You get it out of your head and off of your chest. You also get guidance on how to handle what you are feeling.

    I kept putting all this weight and pressure on myself, covering up how I was really feeling with being so quick tempered. I wanted to take attention off of what I thought people were looking at and make them focus on something else, which was my negative and quick-to-fight attitude. This was the wrong way to go about handling my self-esteem issues. I took all of my frustrations out on other people who had nothing to do with it. When we are going through things sometimes it's easier for us to make it seem like it's everyone else and not really us. We don't really want to deal with the real because it's too painful. But going through the pain is what's going to make you heal. In the end you will be pain free. There is a scripture in the Bible that talks about God giving us beauty for ashes (Isaiah 61:3). What the scripture is really saying is that all the hell and all the pain you have suffered through in life wasn't in vain. Yes, it might have hurt and you never thought you would make it through; but there is going to come a day where God will make it all better! You won't always have that pain. You won't always feel how you feel about life. God bottled up every tear and is waiting to pour them back on us in joy, love and peace. The beauty I have received for my ashes is nothing compared to what I went through. Was it easy? No! Did it hurt? Yes, but to see the hand of God in my life now makes it all worth it. It wasn't until I was in my last years of high school that I became comfortable with myself and accepted the fact that I wasn't ever going to be light skinned. I had to pray that God would show me how to love me. How could I get into a relationship with someone if I first didn't love myself? I couldn't, I had to first know who Ebony was and believe that God created me exactly how he wanted me to be. Now being self-fulfilled is one of the hardest things to achieve because no matter what we always see one flaw. I'm sure even the prettiest person in the world can find something wrong with herself. The key is moving on from it, you have to learn how to work what you have and maximize on what is good about you and beautiful. Let that shine and I promise you the one flaw that you do find becomes smaller and smaller.

In addition, I don't want to sound like I'm bashing the media and the celebrities that are light skinned, because I'm not. They are beautiful in their own rights just like we are. They are exactly what God wanted them to be for the job he destined for them. I think the media now has done a good job of showing a diverse group of women. They have curvy girls, dark girls, skinny girls, and light skinned girls all over. It's not just geared to one audience like it used to be. People are more receptive of darker skin and people are being proud of what they have. Now right beside the magazine covers with Tamar Braxton are covers of Tasha Cobbs and Lupita Nyong'o. BET now does the awards show called *My Black is Beautiful* and I love the message of it. It doesn't matter what shade of black you are everyone is beautiful and everyone is different. I never thought I would be able to be as confident as I am now, but I am. You too can be as confident as you want, once you stop caring about what everyone else thinks about you. Just know that you are who you are for a purpose and walk in that.

Weight

This topic is just as important as skin color because weight plays a huge role in a person feeling beautiful or not. I know it definitely did for me. When I was younger, I was a chubby girl and I always have been. I never was the girl that could go in a store and find clothes right off the rack that fit. I had to go to the bigger sizes and search for what I wanted. I remember going prom dress shopping and I found a dress that I liked but I couldn't try it on because it wasn't in my size it was like a 6 or something. I remember looking at all the other girls in the boutique trying on their gowns and being fitted. In my head I thought, why did I have to be fat? I literally told myself that in my head that day. The lady told me I could have it ordered in whatever size I needed but to me it was deeper than that. Why couldn't I be like everyone else and walk in and try on the dress as is? I have always struggled with self-esteem issues concerning my weight. In grammar school I had my group of friends, but of course I had the kids that were ignorant and wanted to point out my flaw to cover up their own. I'll never forget the day I was in computer class in elementary school and this boy asked me and this other girl did we consider ourselves skinny, thick, or fat. I answered and said well I think I'm thick. The guy and everyone around started laughing at me. Another girl stood up and said, "No I'm thick. You're just fat". I never was one to let them know that they bothered me so I didn't really show any emotion, but my feelings were hurt and I was so embarrassed. It was almost as if they asked the question because they knew I was insecure about my weight. What bothered me was that they were trying to broadcast my insecurities to make themselves feel better about life. I will never understand why people feel the need to put you down to bring themselves up. I dealt with this a long time in grammar school but once again I never told anyone because it was embarrassing to me. It was embarrassing that I was fat and secondly that I was getting made fun of because of it. So for a majority of my years in Grammar school I dealt with all the teasing and the insecurities by myself. I think my mom may have had an inkling that I had weight issues but she never addressed them with me. There were times where I would stand in the mirror, lift my shirt up and suck my stomach in to see how I would look if I were skinnier. I walked around sucking in my stomach because that made me look smaller than I was. When I was in school, I always wanted someone to come to my rescue and kind of stand up for me but no one ever did. I started to feel alone and like I was fighting for the right to just be myself but I was losing that fight. I wanted to be comfortable with myself so bad but I couldn't. The things they were saying about me really had begun to sink in and I was starting to believe them. If you hear that you are fat for so long then eventually you're going to own it and walk in it. That's exactly what happened to me.

Instead of focusing on the things I could do I focused on what I couldn't do. I would get angry because I could never wear a two piece bikini or swimsuit. All the other girls would go the beach and hang out and have on their two pieces and when I went to the beach I had on a one piece. Something so small drove me so crazy; I didn't even feel comfortable around other skinny people in my swimsuit because I felt like they were whispering about me. When in reality, nobody was even thinking about me. My mind had begun to play tricks on me. I was thinking all the time, somebody, somewhere was saying things about me. So because I was so insecure, I started trying to fit in. I developed a mouth like a sailor. Everybody else was cursing like crazy so every other word that came out of my mouth was a curse word. I remember one time in school I called my teacher out of her name because I was trying to act tough like I didn't care about the consequences. If kids weren't going to call me skinny they would think I was a tough fat kid then. Then one of the girls I called my friend went and snitched on me to the teacher to make sure she knew I called her out of her name. When I got home I felt so bad. I knew that was wrong and that I shouldn't have called her out of her name. I remember writing an apology letter but I never gave it to her because of my pride. I had adopted this mentality of trying to do stuff to take away from people talking about my weight. Instead of them saying, "OMG! She's fat! They would say, "OMG! Did you know Ebony did whatever it was. Even in Bible class at my church, when I was in the youth program, I would be so rude and disrespectful to the youth leaders. Even at church I still felt like the big one because I was the big one. Everybody else was smaller than me or just skinny with nice shapes. I would act as I didn't care about anything they were saying because to me it made me feel good. I felt good finally about myself but for the wrong reasons. I was doing rude things and being disrespectful to people I didn't even know - all because of my weight insecurities. Now, some of you might say, "Well your rudeness doesn't have anything to do with your weight"; but it does. People will do anything to take away from what they are really feeling about themselves, because it hurts too much. We don't want to deal with the true feelings we have because it makes us feel weak. It makes you feel like you let the people that were saying these things about you win. But they are winning regardless because they are still making you act out of your character. In my early years of high school, I bullied this one kid so bad for absolutely nothing. I was still a little insecure and needed to have a good rep. I went to Grayslake North in the northern suburbs now it's a primarily Caucasian school with not many minorities. I wanted to have the rep of the big bad girl from Chicago. I wanted people to be afraid of me because if they were then who was going to talk about me? So I set my eye on a target (which actually made me look weak, now that I think back). I looked weak because I knew that this boy was weaker than I was and that he wouldn't retaliate. That is why I chose him. I tried to fight him in class. I put my hands on him and slammed his head into a water fountain, all because I thought I was fat. I feel so bad now about the things I did to people because it was so not even worth it.

The body for a woman starts to change in so many different ways. You start to develop breasts, girls get bigger booties, some girls get fatter and some girls get skinnier. Whatever the case may be for you, you don't really pay it any attention until you reach about 13 or 14 years old and other peers notice. This is the age girls start to feel inadequate and notice if the next girl has something that they don't. It's all about who has the biggest breasts or the bigger booty. Whether you do or don't you are going to get talked about, either way. If you have a big butt, the girls who don't will talk about you and make you feel embarrassed about having a big butt. If you don't have a big butt the girls that do have a big butt will make you feel embarrassed about not having a big butt. It's a lose-lose situation. You are going to get talked about either way. Another thing that makes me angry is that most of the judgment comes from male peers. Of course, as girls we look for acceptance from boys because we don't know any better at this age. We just want to be liked by the opposite sex and if they don't like us, then it causes us to look at ourselves as if we are the problem. When I was in school, I was so jealous of the girls who had a lot of guys that liked them because that wasn't my story. The guys liked the skinny or thick girls that could do and go everywhere; which I couldn't because my mom wasn't playing that with me. I started feeling as if I was missing out on something. For so long I felt like I didn't meet the standard for beauty. More than anything, the guys made me feel fat. They were the main ones talking about me. I got tired of trying to figure out what was wrong with me instead of appreciating everything that was right with me. I learned to love myself no matter what everyone else thought of me, and that I was beautiful in my own right. I decided that people were going to have to get to know me for me and not for my looks. I know I am a good person. I love people to the ends of the earth. I just wanted that in return. I didn't want to be characterized by my weight and not for my personality. Once people get to know me I think they realize that I'm just like them skinny, dark, fat, or whatever the case may be.

It gets to a point where you start to feel sick that you can't be happy with yourself and that you feel less than in society. People will talk about you no matter who you are, or what you look like, it's inevitable in this world we live in.. You have to learn to take the criticism and move on; people will have an opinion whether you look good or bad. You can't lose your confidence every time someone comes and tells you what they think about you. It should actually make you a better person because if they talking about you they could be hating on you which means you have something they want. Beauty comes in all shapes and sizes which means that people need to wake up and stop fighting what just is. They look at a fat person and some people treat them like the scum of the earth. To me it's heartbreaking, because at the end of the day they are still a real person who has feelings. I feel like people have been trying and still trying to fight the acceptance of curvy and thick women being in fashion shows and on magazine covers. People need to evolve with the times and accept the fact that everybody isn't going to be a size 2 and that curvy girls are just as important as skinny girls. I especially love Tyra Banks and what she stands for as a super model. Tyra Banks we all know is beautiful and skinny and she is probably one of the best at what she does. But she doesn't let that go to her head. She always takes a stand about what beauty is. She says that beauty is in so many different shades of color, size, and height. I have seen her interviews and she says that she is making it her life to show and tell young girls that they are beautiful no matter what! I think coming from Tyra Banks this would make girls really stop and listen to what she has to say. She is gorgeous and has the look that most people want, and she doesn't have to say or do anything to try and help make young girls feel beautiful but she does. It helps to know that someone is doing something out of the goodness of their hearts and not because they are being forced to. There are a lot more celebrities that do this as well and I know for me it really helped because; you get to hear it over and over again from different people.

God wants us all to know that he created us how he saw fit for us to be created. Who are we to let people bring us down about how we look? When we allow that to happen we have taken all power from God himself and given it to whoever has you feeling that way. Do you really want to take away the power from the Most High and give it to some knuckle head boy or girl? I know I wouldn't. "for the Lord sees not as man sees; man looks at the outward appearance, but the Lord looks on the heart" (1 Sam. 16:7). I love this scripture because it tells me to only worry about one thing which is the heart. Why should I care if my nose is too big, if I have ugly feet, if my chest is too flat, if my butt is too big, if my hair won't grow, if I'm fat, skinny, short, tall etc. why should I care about those things if God only cares about my heart being right for him? We shouldn't care, and that's the point I want us all to get to because when we get to heaven, it's not going to matter what you look like. All that will matter is if you were saved and if you won souls for Jesus Christ? God made everything on earth beautiful and yes that includes you, no matter who you are.

CHAPTER 4

A Night Out Doesn't Mean Put Out

"Sexual intercourse is a gift that says, do not open until marriage! If you've already unwrapped it, wrap it up again!"

Molly Kelly

Sex is one of those topics that has become a common thing to talk about. Sex is basically everywhere! You have sex in music, on TV, and even in commercials. "Sex sells" is the term we use today to justify why it's in everything. That doesn't make it right, it's just the times we are living in, where everybody follows suit with whatever is selling. It has been taken out of its biblical content which was for husband and wife to reproduce. Now sex is between boyfriends and girlfriends, two people that only want one night stands, between the on again off again boyfriend and girlfriend and in the LGBT community. Why is it given away so easily? Sex is something that the woman was supposed to save for her husband. Not to let everyone test drive it until one man finally decides to put a ring on it. In 1st Thessalonians 4:3 it says "For this is the will of God, even your sanctification that ye should abstain from fornication." I know everyone isn't religious and everybody doesn't read the Bible as they should, but this scripture is clearly self-explanatory, *don't have sex before marriage*. It also says that for your own sanctification, implying to keep your own body, so that you don't get any STD's. There are some people who claim to be real Christians, but they only listen to the parts of the Bible that they choose. They think that by God telling us not to have sex that he is taking away their fun. But in actuality he is trying to save your life. Yes there are condoms to prevent STD's but let's be real some guys don't even like to use condoms while having sex. In the heat of the moment if you're a girl because sometimes all it takes is the right boy to say the right thing in your ear "Baby let's just do it bare, it'll feel better" especially if this is a boy you are serious about you will fall for that trick. By falling for that trick just like that you could have AIDS. That's not to say girls are weak and can be easily brain-washed but because we are women we are emotional creatures already. Sex is an emotional thing once you open that door it's hard to think rationally. God knows all of this so he tries to warn us and save us but we as fleshly people and want to do what we want to do. We don't take heed to the warning.

Alongside getting an STD, you could very well end up pregnant. A baby is a gift from God meant to be shared with a husband and wife. The most common thing now is to see a girl pregnant. It used to be a shock to people but now people are like oh so and so is pregnant and so and so is pregnant, too. I love to hear girls say well God blessed me with this child so it is what it is. Umm yes, he blessed you with the child. The sin isn't in the child, it's in the premarital sex. Most girls that get pregnant don't even have help from their baby's daddy; they end up doing it all alone or with the help of their own mom and dad. Had you waited on your husband, you wouldn't have to worry about all the responsibilities alone. It would be a joint effort. Now you can't even properly love on your child and give what they need because your too mad at the baby daddy. Don't let the child look like the father either, it's going down. Now you don't even want to look at the baby because he reminds you of the mistake you made. You can give the baby up for adoption but when it grows up, the baby could develop a rejection issue. The child will want to know why their biological parents didn't want them. Not having sex before marriage also can save you from a lot of heartache. If you give yourself to someone and then they start acting like they are not interested in you anymore, how broke would you feel? You would realize he only wanted that one thing?

Babies and sex confuses things in your life and makes life much more difficult. You should be focusing on school, getting good grades, graduating and planning for your future. Trying to find a baby sitter so you can go back to school can be challenging.. Getting an education is easier when you don't have the responsibility of trying to take care of someone else. Plenty of people have had babies and gone to school. But if you ask them, I'm sure they will tell you it's not as easy as it seems. Babies need to be fed and changed regularly, and they cry all the time. How can you possibly try and get any work done while taking care of all of that? You will get frustrated and annoyed because it begins to be a lot after a while so you just give up on school, because you can't just give up on your baby.

I am 25 years old and I am a virgin. I made the decision to abstain because premarital sex is a sin. Like I stated earlier, I was raised in church. Secondly, I didn't want to have to worry about giving myself to the wrong person. I want to make sure whoever I lose my virginity to is the man that I would be with for the rest of my life. I didn't want to deal with the drama of having sex and then not hearing from the guy again. I didn't want to deal with getting my emotions involved and then he cheats on me. Remaining a virgin is also a way of showing me who I need to be involved with and who I don't. There have been guys who stopped talking to me as soon as sex came up, because I told them I wasn't having it until I was married. In situations like that, I feel bad because sometimes they were really guys I liked. However, if you can't respect my wishes and my body then I don't need to be with you at all. It gets hard sometimes because you only get older and your body goes through different changes. You start to feel things you didn't before. But as long as you can be strong and fight the urges and keep the goal in mind then you will be fine. I look back and laugh at how people used to talk about me in elementary school, because I couldn't do all of the things they could. My mom wouldn't let me walk the streets and hang out. I couldn't go over to boys' houses. I basically couldn't leave the porch. Now all of the ones who were making fun of me are my age with 2 or 3 kids. I couldn't even imagine having a child at this age. I'm still a baby in my own way at 25 years old. I am spoiled to my mom. So I feel like a baby would come in and take away from me. And as Sweet Brown would say, "Ain't nobody got time for that". I got myself to a point where I didn't care what anyone had to say about me. I know what is right for me and what I want for my life; and it wasn't to be a mom, anytime soon. So I kept my virginity and I'm proud of it. People may try and make you ashamed of being a virgin and feel like something is wrong with you because, you're the only who hasn't done it. But I would rather be the last virgin on this earth, then to be giving my goods to a no-good man who doesn't have a pot to pee in. Sometimes letting people talk is the best thing you can do. You have to show people with your actions why you made the decisions you did about your own life. Being a virgin is a good thing. It takes a strong person to be able to say no and take a stand on such a big subject. In the end, a man will come along and appreciate you for it. When you look around, you may see all these girls that are popular, around here with all the boys. You may be saying, "Well God, where is my man? When is it going to be my turn?" Those boys when they mature and become men, they are going to be looking for the girls like you and I. They will want someone who is pure and has saved herself for one special person. No man wants to wife a girl that everyone has had already. He doesn't feel special in that. How does he know one of his homeboys hasn't hit that already? So ladies please be wise in your decision to have sex and remember that abstaining is the best thing for you and your future.

For some girls no one has never explained this to them for whatever reasons. But if you have already lost your virginity and want to start over, you can. You can never get your virginity back, but you can always take a stand to never have sex again until you are married. God is a merciful and forgiving God. If you pray and ask for forgiveness, He will forgive you and you can start clean from that day forward. Everyone makes mistakes and it's ok if you did, because like I said the flesh is weak. It's how you choose to handle your mistake. If you keep making that mistake over and over, then I question how sorry you really are. But if you really stick to what you said and choose to be celibate until marriage then God will honor that, because He is forgiving and you have changed your ways.

In talking about sex, I questioned if I should talk about oral sex or not and I chose to only because in this day and age it seems to be so popular. I've found that oral sex is popular among most kids who want to remain virgins and use this as an outlet. Oral sex is still sex hence the name "oral sex", just because it's not intercourse doesn't mean that it doesn't count. I don't even know where this kind of just popped up from everybody want to give or receive oral sex, but it did and it is sending mixed signals. This is still sex and shouldn't be shared with just anybody. If that is something you are interested in, then it should be kept as a gift to your husband. People can spread diseases through oral sex as well, and the only way to be 100% safe and clean is to abstain.

My next reason for abstaining would be because sex isn't a way to make someone love you, or show your love to someone else, and make someone want to be with you. A lot of times, girls feel pressure to have sex because they want to show that they are in love with their boyfriend or even committed to the relationship. Sex isn't something that can help you determine these things. You can't sleep with someone because you want to keep them in the relationship. If they are threatening to leave you for the next girl, then you tell them baby bye! No man is worth all of that. He will realize what he gave up and be trying to come back to you. Sex is something that is sacred and shouldn't be determined on false circumstances. It's so important for women to understand that we have the power to determine our futures and how everything goes with the guy you're dealing with. A man can't ever tell you when you should sleep with him because it's not his decision to make. You have the key to the cookie jar don't ever forget that. Men throw their weight around all the time so why shouldn't we do the same thing when it comes to protecting ourselves and our bodies?

Another reason is because sex can't be used as a replacement for the love your parents never gave you. People will walk around with so many holes in their heart. When the right person comes along, he can make you feel the way you wish your parents would have. You may be tempted to keep that person in your life because this is the love and affection you have been searching for. It's like a little kid getting the stuffed animal they have been begging for. Once they finally get it, they will hold on to it for dear life. Same thing goes for attention and love if you grew up without it. A lot of times parents have a lot going on and they tend to focus on giving the child a roof over their head, food on the table, and clothes and shoes. To parents this is their way of showing love to their children. Some parents expect the child to automatically know that they love them. But sometimes you still need to hear it said. Some families don't even really show affection to their children, which causes their child to feel empty. Getting a hug or kiss from your parents growing up really makes a difference in your life. It's another way of showing their love for you. I couldn't imagine growing up not receiving a hug or kiss from my mom or dad. While my dad was alive he always told me how much he loved me. To know that some kids don't get that is mind boggling to me. It's so unfortunate because those girls are the ones that will meet the wrong guy who will give them all the love and affection they have missed out on. If he steps to her the right way she will fall so quickly for him because what he appears to be is so appealing to her. The way he talks to her, kisses her, hugs her, and makes her feel is what will make her want to stay with him. She doesn't care that he eventually will start to realize her vulnerability and play on that. What she does care about is that he makes her feel loved and wanted. While it is disturbing, you have to find a different way to deal with not having those things; because having sex isn't the answer. Sex can't replace a mom or dad. Sex won't rid you of the pain you feel. When you think about it, sex will only make it worse because you're constantly suppressing the real issue with a false cure. You aren't dealing with the part of you that wondered why you never got a hug or kiss from your parents. These things only get better with time and really being able to face your mirror of truth. You should definitely talk to your parents about it. Tell them how you feel and how u felt as a child. Let them explain their perspective. Really listen to what they are saying to you. Sometimes parents don't even know that they messed up in their parenting until you tell them. Be strong enough to take the first steps to do what you have to do to make sure you are ok, because I promise you the answer isn't in sex.

I will be the first to tell you that abstaining from sex has **not** been an easy thing for me. It has been something that I have struggled with for years. I have laid in bed and tried to rationalize with myself why I should just do it and go on with life. Thinking everybody else has already done it. I would tell myself, just go ahead one time and see what it's like, knowing in my heart it was wrong. The voice of the enemy had gotten so strong. What I didn't know is that in my natural life I had left some doors open for the enemy to try and stifle my walk with God in the spirit.

When I was in about 8th grade, girls that I was going to school with had started having sex already. They would come to school and tell us about how it was. Whether they were lying or not I didn't know. They sure sounded like they knew what they were talking about. It made me curious on one hand. And on the other, I felt left out because I could not relate to what they were saying. I so desperately wanted to know and be a part of what it was they were talking about that I started reading adult books that I should not have been reading. These books were full of drama and full of sex. I have always been an avid reader and my guilty pleasure is reality TV. So I actually was reading the books because they were entertaining. I never thought that reading those kinds of books would have taken me down the path that it did. Because the books had so much sex in them, I could now go to school and have something to talk about or at least know what they were talking about on a larger scale. But what I didn't know is that the devil would use my wanting to fit in to try and hinder my walk with God by keeping me locked up in a spirit called perversion. Perversion is a sexual behavior or desire that is considered abnormal or unacceptable. As I was going to school and talking like the other girls now, I started to feel good. I finally knew what they were talking about and although I had never had sex or even kissed a boy, my friends didn't know it. I could talk about kissing and I could talk about different sexual positions that I had learned from reading those books. But the more I read those books the sex parts started to jump out at me on the pages. I would read it once and then read it again and then maybe even read it a 3rd time. Something about it had captivated my mind body and soul. Each time I read those words on the page, I wanted to know more about it. I wanted to know how I could feel that same feeling the writer had written about. The fact that I was curious and wanted to experience that feeling was all that the enemy needed to taint me. All he is ever looking for is a small crack so that he can slip through it and create an even bigger hole to destroy you. So because he knew I was interested a little bit, he allowed me to be in the wrong place at the wrong time, hearing the wrong conversation. I was at school and girls were talking about sex again, but this time they were talking about masturbation. Now here I am not even really knowing what it is or how to do it but I heard a girl say that you just touch yourself and relax. All that day, I started to try and figure out how I could masturbate and not be caught, because I still lived with my mom. So I decided that I would do it at night, when she and everyone else was asleep. I started to do this on a regular. I felt like it was fine because I felt like I was getting the feeling like the people in the books, but I wasn't having sex. I thought I had got one over on God. So every time I read a book that had a sex scene in it, I would read the pages and masturbate to it because it had become a part of my life. I had no idea that I was creating a monster on the inside of me that later on would cause me so much agony. I continued to enjoy what I thought was fun until one day I got caught with one of those books at my cousin's house. She was so mad that I was reading those books. Not only was I reading them, I had exposed her daughter to them, as well. She took my book and gave it to my mom and told on me. I was ANGRY with her but she did not care at all, because she knew the doors that I was opening. My mom took and hid the books from me. I had no way of getting my material anymore. But since I am a visual person, I could visualize what was going on. So I started to playback scenes in my head that I read and I started learning how to have memory recall so that I could still masturbate even though my books were gone.

The enemy wanted to keep me stuck in sin and wanting more. One option was gone but he quickly provided another one for me to use. I thought it was amazing. Growing up, we got cable pretty late (meaning everyone had already had it and then my mom and grandmother finally decided to get it). What they didn't know was that they needed to censor some of the channels, because after hours on certain channels inappropriate and explicit things came on TV. As I would scroll through the channels, I would notice that the later it got, the more sensual the programs became. Kissing scenes would be more and more passionate, nudity would become a little bit more and things were way sexier. This automatically intrigued the perversion in me. The crazy part was I started to take risks. Earlier I told you that I shared a room with my mom and brother. So while they were sleeping I started to watch porn on TV. I would watch pornographic TV shows and movies (I will not mention the names because I don't want to open any doors for you all). Whenever my mom would move or turn over, I would change the channel because I never wanted to get caught; but I didn't want to stop either. As I played with this spirit of perversion, I found myself going deeper and deeper into it, more than I ever thought I would be. Remember, this started as me wanting to fit in at school, to reading books, to watching porn on tv. From there I started watching porn hub on my phone. Now I had my fix in a way that it was accessible to me at all times. I found myself going to masturbate at the most random times. What started as a fun thing had now become an addiction and I couldn't stop it on my own. During this time, I was getting older of course and I started to deepen my personal relationship with God. As I learned more about Him, His ways and laws, I started to feel bad that I was stuck in perversion. I had learned enough about God to know that what I was doing was wrong and that I was dealing with a real spirit. But now, the devil plagued me with fear, guilt and shame! How could I open up and tell people what I was dealing with and they not judge me or look at me like I was nasty? I decided that I would not allow God to deliver me, but that I would just deliver myself and stop on my own. After multiple failed attempts, I soon realized that fighting the spirit of perversion was not up to me. The voice of it had become bigger than I was. It was a giant and I was a mouse. There was no way I would be able to stop. I came to the conclusion that I would die in it and take this secret to the grave with me. There was something on the inside of me that knew I needed help and that I needed to stop. I did try to stop several times but it was like something would over power me and I would always do it just one more time. I started to feel dirty and shameful because here I am in church trying to live a holy life and behind closed doors I am secretly addicted to masturbation and pornography. It was a constant battle within me and I kept coming up short, on the losing end. If someone would have told me, I would have ended up fighting this kind of spirit, from me reading those books, I would have never picked them up. The enemy is very smart and clever. He knows how to take our innocence and use it against us for his evil plans. The longer I stayed in turmoil over feeling stuck in the sin, it gave the enemy more room to talk to me about who I was and who I wasn't. The devil would tell me, God doesn't love me because he doesn't like that I masturbate and that I watch pornography. The devil would tell me that people will judge me if I open up and share what I'm going through. At the same time he is telling me to feel bad and be ashamed. I was in mental torment over this and all I wanted was to be free!

My true freedom came when I made the decision that I would live for God and that I would die for God. God had become my one and only. I decided that I wasn't going to live a double life anymore, being one way in front of people and then living in perversion when people are not around. As I began to pray, I asked him to take that thing away from me. He did just that. I began to pray and ask God that his holy conviction would fall on me every time I listened to the voice of the enemy. God began to do just what I asked. He honored my request. Here is the thing I want you to grab, I started watching porn and masturbating when I was a young girl. Here I stand now 25 years old and every now and then I have to check the devil and tell him, "Nope I've passed that test already". I will not go backwards. There's a scripture in the Bible that talks about when a person gets delivered from something, the devil will try and come back to see if he can get back in. If he can, he brings along with him seven spirits stronger than they were before. There were times where I thought I was delivered and the enemy would come and tell me to look at something and I would. Then there I go doing it again! Each time I fell for it, I felt like it was getting worse and worse. And according to this scripture it was. It took me years to break this spirit off of me but once I did, I decided I would never go back! There were serious steps involved in me breaking the spirit of perversion, I had to change a lot of things I did and liked to do. For one, I had to be very mindful of what I allowed to enter into my ear and eye gates. Meaning that all the sexual music I liked to listen to I could no longer listen to, because it fed a part of the perversion for me. We listen to music all day and we don't think that it has any effect on us and how we react naturally, but it does. Whatever you choose to feed your soul is what you will reproduce in the earth, so if all you listen to is sexual music and love songs your mind will eventually cause you to act on what you have taken in. Same thing goes for the violent rap that everyone listens to. And then we wonder why the world is in the state that it is with all the killings. Because of this, I started to intentionally change the station when something played that I felt like I didn't need to hear. Also, I started being mindful of what I watched. The same thing applies to your eyes, whatever your eye gate consumes is what you feed your soul. As hard as it was for me, because I love reality TV and music so much. But through prayer and fasting, I was able to pull through and overcome this demon. I never want to be stuck in perversion again because it was a hard time in my life, especially going through it all by myself. I just recently opened up about it to my godmother and Apostle who showed me nothing but love and support about it. I needed to bring in others because this is something that I still battle, today! I don't act on it anymore, but that doesn't mean the thoughts don't cross my mind; because they do. The devil is always lurking and waiting to find a crack where he can come in and raise a mess. I, at this point know, that some things you can't do alone. you need the strength, prayers, and the fight of others to help you get and stay through. So now I know that they pray for me and that they are standing with me in prayer, concerning not going backwards. Why did I bring all of that up? Because when I started watching porn and masturbating, I thought that I had found a way around having sex but still getting my fix. I thought I had got one over on God because I was still a virgin and not having sexual intercourse. But I was wrong because even masturbation is wrong because the Bible tells us to have dominion over our own bodies in 1st Thessalonians verse 3 and 4. Also the Bible says that in Colossians 3:5 that we are to put to death whatever belongs to our earthly nature. Of course, people take these scriptures to mean what they want but to me it's clearly saying that we should not be doing anything outside of honoring our bodies. And masturbation is a dishonor to the body.

CHAPTER 5

SISTERHOOD

"Let's not only build ourselves, but each other as well"
Ebony Steward

Being a girl is such a privilege and an honor in my opinion. I think being a girl gives us a power in the world that no one can take from us. We have the power to bare children when we are married. We also have the power to take a stand about what will and will not take place in our lives. Coming from a world where women didn't have any control and had to go through men for everything, I think we have done alright for ourselves. Women are getting educated. More women everyday are getting their degrees and becoming lawyers, doctors, and even getting jobs in sports. As a people we have come so far and should be celebrating what women are doing today and what women will accomplish in the future. We should be paving a way for our daughters and grandchildren to come in and not have to struggle as much as we did growing up. Given all of these beautiful things women have accomplished, why is that we bring each other down more than anybody else? Women are some of the most jealous people. I will never understand how you can be a woman and not celebrate another woman doing something great. Just as a woman knowing the history, you should be elated when a woman gets her degree. Celebrate when she gets a job at a huge company and later becomes the CEO of that company. Applaud her when she buys her first house and car with her own money she worked so hard for. Instead we give each other the side eye, and start whispering about how she thinks she is better than everybody else. When in reality, all she trying to do is make a better life for herself, just as we all should be. Being envious of someone is just a sign of your own insecurities popping up. It's the number one signal to show you still have this little thing you need to work on inside of you. There's really no reason to be jealous of anyone or anything that they have. You, too, can have it. You just have to put in the work. My pet peeve is when we can see someone doing something well, they're on their grind, but we sit back rolling our eyes and bad mouthing that person. We should be following in their footsteps going to school, looking for a good job, and trying to be the best we can be, instead of being a hater. You can't bring yourself up by bringing someone else down. You won't get anywhere in life like that. The Bible says that when one celebrates we all should celebrate, and that's how it should still be. In rejoicing for someone else you might just get your own blessing. How will God be able to bless you if your heart isn't right? You are walking around carrying all kind of hatred, jealousy, and some of everything else in your heart, God can't bless mess he is not the author of confusion.

I look at all these shows that I watch on TV today and although they are very entertaining, they are all so crazy. There are a bunch of grown women who have nothing better to do than to fight each other. I used to love looking at Bad Girls Club, but when I tell you some of those women have nothing better to do than to fight each other. It's ridiculous. The show is supposed to bring 7 or 8 bad girls together from whatever city they decide to tape the show in. They put them all in one house to live together for a certain amount of weeks, and hopefully bring about a change in the end. Now, if you bring together eight of any city's baddest girls you are for sure to have a hot mess. They are obviously called bad for a reason. They don't have a care in the world. They think it's ok to pick up a bottle or whatever is in the vicinity at the time and throw it, or hit the next girl over her head with it. They go out to the clubs all the time and pick up random guys, bring them home and then have sex with them. Half the time, they get kicked out of the club for fighting anyway. But if they are lucky enough to stay the whole night at the club, they are drunk and turning up. House rules are that you aren't supposed to fight and if you do then you have to leave the house, but that doesn't stop them from fighting. I remember watching one season and two girls were fighting and all in each other's faces. One girl actually opened her mouth and spit in the others girl's face. I'm sure we all know that spiting on someone is the absolute worst thing you can ever do to someone. I was so disgusted that she had done that because she was on television. Even if she does mature and turn over a new leaf, people will always remember her for spitting in that girl's face.

Why are they so angry with one another? Why can't they actually try and get along and make the best of the time they are going to be there? They put each other down based off of who has what type of purse or shoes on, who is intelligent and who isn't, or who wears the better outfit. All of those things are not even what's important. I don't care what you have on or what shoes you wear, I care about your deeper issues. I want to get to the root of what is making you act the way you are. Those are the things we should care about. No one goes around trying to fight the world, and put down everybody else to make themselves feel better for no reason. There has to be some deep-rooted issues there. If they took the time out to sit and get to know one another, then they would probably end up helping each other. Instead girls come on the show looking to be the leader and looking to see who is the weakest girl in the house. They target that person to bother. When a stronger more dominant person picks on a weaker individual, it makes the stronger one look weak. You already know that the weaker one isn't going to fight you, or have a confrontation with you, because that's not their character. For you to continue to pick on them makes you the dumb one because you are just using your own strengths to belittle the weaker one. Why not build up the weaker one and help them find a backbone? Uplifting each other would make us stronger and make it difficult for men to tear us down because they would know that we will all stick together in the end.

I really want to encourage you to be the person that I know you can be. I'm not saying that you will get along with every woman you come in contact with, because you won't. Everybody is different and has different personalities, some will click and some won't. That doesn't mean that you have to hate that person and can't be happy for them when good comes their way. God says for us to love our brother and sister in Christ and that is what we should do.

How about we help each other build our legacies instead of watching the same person struggle time after time. We look down on other women and girls trying to get a foot through the door, as if we have never needed the same help. Once you make it to your destination, you should be coming back to get others and see who is trying to make it where you have. Who can you lend a hand to? If we stop being so uppity, we can look at one another and see we are fighting the same battle and not be characterized into a group of statistics for women. Just because you made it to your goal safe and sound doesn't mean the next person will. They could be fighting all kinds of other personal problems you know nothing about. Let's learn to be a sister to our fellow peers and not an enemy.

I have a cousin named Brittney. We are all proud of her because she is now in college and playing basketball in Canada. She started out playing ball in high school and was playing on the freshman team. She worked really hard to make a name for herself on the team. She did it with dedication and hard work. She knew nothing was going to be handed to her. If she wanted it, she had to go after it. She competed all over Lake County and in other areas as well. Now we see her name in newspapers and all over. She has a younger sister named Brandi who is following in her shoes and playing ball like she is. Brandi has mastered her skill just like her sister did. When she goes to high school, she will attend the same school her big sister went to. But because her sister has paved the way for her, the school's coach wants her to play on the varsity team with seniors. Who does that? I have never heard of a freshman coming in and playing straight on the team with the seniors all because of the name your sister left behind. The point I'm trying to make is that Brittney paved the way for Brandi, so she didn't have to struggle and fight as hard as she did. Now Brandi's walk will be a little easier and she owes it all to her sister. Brittney couldn't be happier for Brandi. There's no drama or jealousy at all. And that's the way it should be; because they are sisters for one and secondly, because they are both girls and Brittney should be proud that she was able to help her sister by leaving a legacy behind.

Another thing women need to work on is telling ourselves we don't need each other in our lives. Women sometimes tend to be very catty and keep up a lot of drama. So for some women it's easier to surround themselves with a lot of men because it keeps down the drama and makes life easier for them. I was definitely a fan of this idea because I have had my fair share of drama with girls. It was pointless and tiring so I had decided that I would make friends with a lot of guys to keep a low profile. Although I was in the drama, I hated it because it got to a point where I couldn't even figure out why I was in it. So I tried to shut out the female world, all except for my female cousins. A lot of women take this route because when we look at men, they don't have as much drama as we do. Yes they fight with each other, but they don't hold grudges. They can have an argument and make up in a matter of 5 minutes. They tend to let things go quicker than a woman. It's merely because of their make-up. Men weren't made to go around arguing, yelling and being so catty, like women are. Why is it in our nature more than theirs? I will never know. (You'll have to take that up with God.) But since it is, we try to find outlets to avoid the drama, which is a way of just running from an issue. Every time you get around a group of women, it shouldn't have to be drama. We should all be able to co-exist with one another. Unfortunately this is a stereotype women have and we seem to live up to it all the time. We give people the satisfaction of being right about us, because of shows like Basketball wives, and RHOA. We watch these shows and we laugh, and it's very entertaining for us. However, it's very sad that the network needs to bring together a group of women to fight to get ratings. We may think, "Well they are getting paid, so they're good". But it's not good. A check isn't worth your character. Women who think they can run from the issue of being friends with other women soon find themselves running into a conflict, even with the men. A man can keep you in good company for a little while. Men can be just as much fun as women can be. But, you will never get the feeling of familiarity with a man that you will have with a woman, for obvious reasons.

I started my menstrual cycle at the age of 13, so for 12 years I have had bad cramps. I cramp so much that some days all I can do is lay in my bed on the heating pad and watch TV or sleep. I can talk about this to my friends or to my cousins because they get it and they understand the power of the cramps, but guys don't. Guys are gone tell you to pop a couple of Midol or ibuprofen and keep it moving but in the midst of a cramp, that's not something you want to hear. No man is going to be able to sympathize with you about your cycle or cramps or anything of that nature because obviously they don't go through it. These are the things that bring women closer together. By being able to relate to something as little as cramps opens the door to be able to relate on a deeper level. But if we don't ever deal with other women, how will we know what relationships could come out of that? One of my newest favorite shows to watch was The Real with Tamar, Lonnie, Adrianne, Tamera, and Jeanie. I love this show for multiple reasons. They are a diverse group of women who show that they can work together, well. They are all very opinionated, but they don't let each other's opinion cause them to hate each other or even stop them from being able to work together. You will hear them say all the time in the beginning they were intimidated by each other. They weren't sure what they were going to get. Now, you look at them (season two of their show just came out) and they are all like real friends. It breaks the stigmatism that women can't work together and I think that is awesome!

Some of us need to check ourselves and make sure that we aren't the problem in the situation. We need to make sure that we don't bring the drama to the situation. If every time you're in a group of women, there is a conflict, you're the common denominator. So unknowingly you might be the problem. If you are, that's ok because like I said you might not even know it. But it's important that you figure out what is in you that makes it hard for you to get along with other women. It could be a childhood trauma. When you were younger, you could have been bullied by a group of girls or a female family member taunted you. Typically when you have a childhood trauma it rolls over into your adulthood. You start to view people differently based on who it was that made your childhood traumatic for you. In high school, you have your few girls that you consider your friends or your best friends. You guys hang out and talk on the phone all the time, and then suddenly you start to feel left out. You're calling them but they aren't calling you. When you do talk it's almost like pulling teeth to get a comment out of them. You see pictures on their Instagram of them hanging out, but you weren't invited. They kicked you out the group for no apparent reason and you still thinking you all were still friends. That would be traumatic for me because I consider myself to be a good girlfriend to people I call my friends. We know how the high school clique thing goes, one minute you're in, and the next you're out. But what many don't realize is there are people out there who really value their friendships, and they are really affected by the whole 'in one minute, out the next' thing. It's not as simple to you as it is to them because you have been a good friend to them and to not have it returned is devastating. If this has happened to you, then you may eventually start to not trust women because you have a wall up. You build the wall to protect yourself and your emotions from being hurt again. When you get older, you may have coworkers who all go out for drinks after work. It makes it difficult for you to want to build that personal relationship with them because, you keep having a flashback to when you were in high school. You can socialize with people but you don't want to share any of your personal self with them. You think they will turn around and use it against you. You were vulnerable once and opened your heart to women and they stepped on it. They left you with a bad taste for all women in your mouth.

It also may look easier for you to distance yourself from all women because when you are talking to men, you can avoid the uncomfortable conversations with women. Men usually talk about sports, cars, jobs, etc. They rarely ever talk about their girlfriends or wives with other men unless they are asking for advice. If you are present, I'm sure they will avoid the relationship topic. If you're like me, you like sports and cars so for you talking with guys about those things would be easy and fun. Whereas when you're talking to a woman, the conversation is a lot different. It's way more emotional and sentimental. Women like to talk about their families, work, and just things that have happened over the years. We go deeper in a conversation because that's how we build relationships. So what if all of these things are going terribly wrong for you? What if you and your parents aren't getting along, you guys are arguing about nothing all the time? If you have a boyfriend, you guys can't get it together, either. School isn't going how you would like. It almost seems like everything that could possibly go wrong has. You are not going to want to talk about those things to somebody else. That's a lot to have to go through all at once. It will almost seem like it's easier to just avoid it then deal with it. So you distance yourself from another woman and find friendship in men. Men aren't going to be sitting around talking about your issues, so you get to avoid it all. It's almost like an escape for you because it takes your mind off of it. But truth is talking to another woman about it can really help you get through it. Nine times out of ten, they have been through the same things or they are going through the same thing. You have a listening ear that totally understands and gets your perspective of things because you are both females. It's something about knowing that you have that one person that gets you and where you are coming from. You don't get that all the time because your parents don't understand because of the age difference. Your boyfriend won't understand because he is male and he's going to think you're overreacting. But a woman will talk to you and make you feel like you are being heard and that you are not crazy for thinking and feeling the way you are.

When you grow older, you start to act more and more like your mom, and it will terrify you. A woman is the only person that will understand that because she will be going through it, too. We love our moms to death and we hope to be half of what they are when we reach their age. But there are some things we don't want to inherit that unknowingly we will. When we do it or say it, we will be like OMG that was not me, that was my mother. Then the state of shock kicks in and we freak out. When we were younger, that's the very thing we said we would never do or say. You tell your husband and he doesn't care because to him his mom is perfect, and so is yours. He doesn't care what you said you would never do or say when you were younger. To him you're overreacting and being dramatic. That doesn't take away how you feel. These are girlfriend times because this would be something you all have in common. Every woman at some point or another will experience this (sorry lol). When you have children, you want to be able to share your birthing experiences with your girlfriends and talk about the differences in labor you had. Will you ever do it again? Maybe you will talk about how your husbands fainted at the sight of the baby crowning. You can call your friends up and tell them about the cute boy you saw. He came and said hey to you and now you guys have a date on Friday. You build relationships when you can relate and have these things in common with another woman.

Now, in order to be able to have friends you have to first know how to be a good friend. As much as we say we don't want friends, we all do. You can have your family to talk to, but at the end of the day you also want that girlfriend. But the friendship can't be built on one side, if you want a friend to be honest, loyal, and there for you when you need them to be, you have to be all those things in return. The friendship should be 50/50 because you both have to put forth an effort to make it work. I think a lot of times girls fall out or can't get along because they don't know how. This can go back to them not having a mom in their life. You learn qualities on how to be a friend from your mom because, she is a woman, she gets it and she has already been through it. If you are never taught how to have and build friendships then it will be something that doesn't come easy for you, and you will struggle in this area.

The online definition of the word friend is "A person whom one knows and with whom one has a bond of mutual affection, typically exclusive of sexual or family relations". A friendship is a bond that you form with someone over time. A lot of people (and I am also guilty of doing this) meet someone, hang out a few times, talk on the phone and then that's your best friend. People are so hungry for friendships that they don't take the time out to get to know a person and see if that is even someone you want to be your friend. Just because you guys hang out all the time doesn't mean that you are friends. Just because you talk on the phone for hours doesn't mean you all are friends. I made this mistake in my life several times. I called people my friend and they weren't my friend. I have been hurt so many times by people I have called my friend, all because I used the word, too loosely. I thought that my friends were who I had the most fun with, who I talked to all the time, and who I hung out with the most. But boy was I wrong. I learned the hard way that I didn't have any friends. I had all "associates." I was a friend to them. I was there for them when they called me crying. I was there for them when they wanted to vent. I was there for them when it was their birthdays and they wanted to celebrate. The hurtful thing was they weren't there for me when I needed them most. I held them at a higher regard than they held me. If I call someone my friend then they are my friend and you become like family to me. I would do anything for my friends that I can. When you don't get that in return, it makes you look at the situation in a different light. It took me literally 4 or 5 years to really figure out what a friend was. What they were doing to me was not being a friend they were just being associates. It hurt my feelings, but honestly I don't regret it because I never want to live life with a bunch of regrets. If I hadn't gone through the hurt, I wouldn't know what a real friend looks like. I know now what I want in a friend and what I don't want in a friend. As I had time to think and reflect on everything that happened, I realized that I was choosing friends that I had nothing in common with. I absolutely believe God put them all in my life for a reason but only he knows what that reason is. All of the people I would talk to were kids who drank, smoked, were having sex, and liked to party. I never liked to do anything of these things at all. I am a virgin so we couldn't relate on that end. I have never smoked so I couldn't relate on that end. I chose to drink once in my life. I was about 18 years old. I went over to someone's house and they were giving us drinks and foolishly I accepted one and I drank it. I will not sit here and say that I was pressured into doing something because ultimately it was my decision to take a stand and say whether I would drink or not. I fell into the temptation and I did drink. The consequences from it made me feel so bad that I never had another drink until I was legally allowed to. So I couldn't go out and drink with my friends because that was something I wasn't interested in. All we could do was go out to eat or to the movies or something. I have never been a huge party goer because it doesn't excite me. I like to have fun just like the next person but going to kick backs, and partying just wasn't fun for me. I knew there was going to be smoking and drinking and I didn't want to be in that environment. We had nothing in common to even base a friendship off of, which is why it didn't last. They may have thought I was being stuck up, but I wasn't. I was just being me and they didn't really understand me as an individual.

A friend should be a person that you build a bond with, over the years. You guys talk and hangout often enough to get to know things about each other. You should have some things in common that you all can relate to. You're not going to have all of the same things in common, which is fine but the differences shouldn't tear you apart. You should be able to work through them and still remain friends. A friend will remember the significant things in your life: birthday, graduation days, etc. Out of all of the people I called my friends, none of them knew the day my dad died or even cared enough to ask. So when that day rolls around, they aren't there to comfort me and make sure I am ok. To me those are the things that build true friendships. Most people think it's the one that will buy you this and buy you that, but it's not. What is important is who is there for you when you are crying your eyes out. You want someone there for you when you celebrate your accomplishments in life. They should be there genuinely because they are proud of you and want what's best for you. They don't get jealous when good things come your way; but they aren't there to try and use you either. A friend is someone that you know you can bring around your man and she doesn't try and get with him behind your back. A friend is someone who you can call on in the middle of the night and talk to and they will stay up and pray with you. A friend pushes you to do better and doesn't let you settle for less when they see your potential and know you can do better. A friend is someone who can tell you the-honest-to-God truth. You can receive it because you know it's coming from a good place. A lot of times people don't want their friends to be honest with them because they don't want to hear the truth. But a person is not your friend if they can't tell you their honest opinion about a situation. They should feel open and free enough to be honest with you and tell you about yourself. I am 25 years old and I still haven't found a real true friend outside of family and people I go to church with. I used to envy people who had found true friends because I wanted it so badly. I'm young, I don't want to sit in the house all the time and do nothing. But I had to realize there's a timing and season for everything. Once I had my feelings hurt, I was ready to shut out the outside world and just be by myself. That's very unrealistic. I can't sit in my room all day and do nothing for the rest of my life. I had to get myself to a place where I was ok with being alone and know that God was my friend. If I wanted to talk, I could talk to him. If I needed to cry, I could cry to him. I pray every day that God would send me true friends and although He hasn't done it just yet I know that He is working it out in my favor. Friends will come into my life. Sometimes we don't understand why God has us on the path that He does, but it's not for us to understand. It for us to just walk and say, "Yes God whatever you are doing in my life, I accept it and I obey." We constantly try and go against God and what he is doing until we realize after all the fighting we have done, nothing has changed. I don't understand why God let everyone I thought was my friend stab me in the back. He has allowed me to be lonely because I don't have any friends. I don't understand it, but I have learned to not question God and I do know that everything he does is for a reason. He has my best interest at heart. As crazy and lonely as it may seem, I trust God and I know he has a plan for me and my life. So whatever road he has me on, I'll walk it with grace.

As I wait for God to send me friends, I learned to use what was around me instead. I thank God for my cousin Brianna, my 1st Godsister, Kezia and the other sisters that have been added! These girls have been my friends. I know I can call each of them and tell them my deepest darkest secrets and they will go nowhere but from my mouth to their ears. I can call them my friends because I have gone through so much with each of them. We all have a bond that can't be broken. I can relate to each of them in so many ways. Brianna and I are six months apart. I'm older, but she still doesn't listen to me (lol). She was born in California and later moved to Japan because her dad was in the navy. When she came back to Illinois, we didn't really know each other, because we hadn't seen much of each other. When she came back here in 2006, she was only 12 years old. It was weird because she was so shy and quiet. However, I was not shy and quiet, so I didn't think we were going to have a lot in common. But I started calling Brianna and talking to her on the phone nearly every day. We became best cousins and we hated being apart from each other. We would get mad at our parents if they told us we couldn't go to each other's houses. One time, Brianna wanted to spend the night at my house in the summer and her mom told her no. We got so angry at her and were pouting and having a hissy fit. I ended up leaving and going home and getting an attitude with my mom because Brianna's mom said no. About 30 minutes later, I heard a knock at the door and it was Brianna. She had pouted to her grandmother and her grandma told her mom to let her spend the night at my house. She did. We were so happy.

As we got older, our relationship started to go through tests, just like any other relationship. Me and Brianna would fight and argue over things that people had either put in our heads or because of things that had personally happened between the two of us. I can remember she and I almost coming to blows once and not speaking on several occasions. I think me and Brianna must have argued and not spoke to each other at least a thousand times. I remember crying and trying to figure out what had happened to us because we went from being connected at the hip to almost hating each other. What I didn't realize was that we were getting older and becoming adults and we didn't know how to deal with each other, anymore. We weren't little girls anymore and we had to learn how to talk and treat each other like the adults we were. I am the type of cousin that If I have gone through something then I think you should listen to me and what I have to say because I am telling you how it's going to end up. I wanted her to heed all of my warnings because I didn't want her to have to go through certain things. So if she didn't listen to me then I took it personally and was angry because I felt my opinion was disrespected. She, on the other hand, felt as though I didn't respect her and that I treated her in a sense like she was naïve and didn't have any street smarts. Our relationship suffered for a long time and we didn't trust each other at all. Now that we are 25 and 24 we have come a long way. We don't see eye to eye on everything, but we can sit down and have a conversation about it and work it out. We may not get it the first time because we are both very stubborn; but we come around a lot sooner than we used to. We get along so much better now. I think it's because we learned to accept each other for who we are and not try and change the other person, or fight their battle for them. We are closer than ever before and I love her to death. There is absolutely nothing I wouldn't do for her. Kezia is what I like to call my walking diary. She knows literally everything about me; good, bad, and indifferent. What I love about her most is that she doesn't judge me. She knows all of my secrets and I have never heard anything that I have ever told her come back from anyone. Kezia and I started building a relationship when I needed her the most. I was going through a lot in my life and I needed a safe place to release it. I thank God for her being in my life. She has shown me more than she ever knows she has. The way she forgives people and the way she loves people is remarkable! She has the heart of Christ and it shows every day. She has the strength of a lion and the power to endure so much. I have always wanted a sister because I am the only girl. When I met her, I can truly say she became the best big sister a girl could ever dream of. I literally could not imagine her not being in my life. Whether its laughing, crying, or praying for one another, I know she has my back and my best interest at heart. And I will always be there for her, no matter what. Now my other sisters are my girls because they accept me. I am a lot to handle at times, but I know they love me and accept me, flaws and all. Jaime, I actually made the mistake of prejudging her before I even got to know her, because that's what we girls do sometimes. I had told myself I wasn't going to like her and she wasn't going to like me. We would never have anything in common. Boy, was I wrong. Jaime and I actually laugh all the time at how much she and I have in common. We both lost our dads when we were 13 years old. Her dad's birthday is one day after my dad's birthday, and we have dealt with some of the same issues in life. What I learned from my relationship with Jaime is to never judge a book by its cover. You will never get the full message from the cover. You have to actually open the pages and see what the story is about. Kristin and Lauren are sisters who became like sisters to me. I love these 2 because whenever we get together its nothing but a laughing party. We all try to make it a priority to spend time together which typically means we kick Kristin's husband and her kids out of the house. We all come over for a girl's night. We eat, talk, cry, laugh, and just open up to one another because we know it's a safe place.

Masika is actually another cousin of mine. Our relationship has just blossomed into something special, especially coming from where it used to be. I love Masika because we can play and crack jokes with each other all day long. But what I love most about her is the strength that I'm not even sure she knows she has. Her story from not being saved to now living her life for Christ. She makes me see that I shouldn't lose hope in anything but that everything happens in the timing of God. As time has gone on the lord has added other special women in my life and sisters whom I love dearly!

These women are my friends and I love them, my life would not be the same if they were not in it. The lesson I learned in having them is that God will surround you with people that you need in your life right when you need them. Having them made me realize that I shouldn't focus on who I don't have but thank God for who I do have. These women will forever be in my life even when I am a well-known author and on the New York Times Best Seller's List (prophetic decree) because they have been here for me in the times when I didn't have anything. They have supported me in everything I've done. I love the fact that we can just be real with one another. They might not tell me everything that I want to hear, but they tell me what I need to hear. We don't always agree on things but we have a mutual respect for each other. If one of us makes a mistake, then we are all there to pick the other one up. I pray for them and I know that they pray for me! I'm grateful to God for allowing all our paths to cross.

CHAPTER 6

The New You

What a journey this has been for you! We have walked through some of the most uncomfortable things there is to possibly deal with to help you become a better person. Just by reading the book, you have already begun to do the work and have taken the first steps. This walk you are on will not be easy. But it is a walk you should most definitely take. It will make you stronger in the end. We hear people who say all the time that they want to change this and they want to change that about themselves. But how many people actually put in the work? We expect God to come in and do everything because He is God. If He wanted to, yes, He could do that. But that's not how He works. God wants us to come to Him and ask Him what are the broken areas of our lives. After He shows you, because He will definitely show you, then it's up to you to start doing the necessary things to change. Praying that God would break the spirit of anger off of you isn't going to happen if every time somebody pushes your buttons, you react with anger. I had to learn this myself, the hard way. I was so angry for so many different reasons. I asked God to change me and I believed that He would, but I didn't act like it in the natural.

If the lady at Popeye's forgot to put my hot honey butter biscuit in my bag, I was angry and ready to call Popeye's and get the lady in trouble. When I got my license, I hated driving behind slow drivers and I hated people who just forced their way into a lane. I would get so angry and lay on the horn or I would call them stupid, idiots, fools or whatever. I can imagine God in heaven looking down at me saying "Daughter, you aren't ready girl. You can't even pass this simple test. What's going to happen when I send the lady who is going to curse your mother out, or that's gone call you out of your name?" I, more than likely, would fail that test because I don't play about my mama. He starts us out small to test and see how ready we are. If you keep failing the minor tests then he knows he can't send you the real big test because you might be praying for bail money. The Bible says faith without works is dead. If you have faith that God will break whatever it is off of you, but you're not working towards it, that's dead. You can't have all the faith in the world and not put any action to it. If I pray for God to break the spirit of anger off of me, then when somebody irritates me, I have to learn how to not react. The key is I have to be intentional about doing it. Of course, my first reaction will be anger if someone provokes me because that's the normal for me. But in the heat of the moment, making a cautious decision to not react negatively is what starts to make the change. The Bible says be angry but sin not. It's ok to be angry because sometimes in life things just happen. But the sin comes in what you do when you're angry (which was my issue). I have a sharp tongue. I will get angry and say something that will have you crying to your mama. I knew that about myself. So I used that as my defense a lot. However, I was wrong because I was sinning. What I should have done was prayed. Then when my test came, I should have been mature enough to turn and walk away and not give the devil any satisfaction.

This is the walk that will truly change your life. You grow spiritually, the more you pray and spend time with God. You also grow naturally as you mature to a new level when you move from anger to not letting little things bother you. You brush them off.

While you are on this journey, it may feel like it is getting lonely. You may think that the people who were there for you aren't there anymore. When you look to your left, you don't see your best friend. When you look to your right, you don't see your boyfriend. God will remove the distractions in your life to get you to the place he wants you. I am going through my journey still and it gets lonely sometimes. We are young and of course we want to hang out and have fun. I can remember having all these people around me that I thought were my friends. One by one, they slowly started falling out of my life. I thought I had two good friends left, and then they left me and I felt so alone and depressed. But little did I know that is exactly where God wanted me because he had a work for me to do. Now I know it was to write this book to tell my story. I couldn't figure out why I was going through so much and why everything seemed to be happening to me. But it's in those places when we are broken, God says ok now I have her in a place to hear me. I have cried many times on this journey, I have even been suicidal on this journey, but I have also had some good days on this journey. But I can promise you I have never been in a better place spiritually in my entire life. This time something just clicks and I get what God has been trying to show me for so many years before. I get why I go through what I go through. I get why I cried so many nights. My trials and tribulations are not for me. They are for my brother and my sister. Each one of us goes through things so that we can be used of God to share our testimony of how God brought us out. It may get stressful and yes, you may want to quit. But you can't. If you quit, how are the ones coming up under you going to know how to withstand tough times? They need to see and know that you made it out. So surely they can make it out. We get so wrapped up in what God is doing in our own lives that we forget what He is trying to do in someone else's life. Someone once told me that the weight of God's glory was upon my life and that meant I wasn't weak and that I could take a lot. If God placed His glory on me, I know for sure he has placed it on some of you. You are overcomers and mighty powerful women of God. If your situation doesn't look good, don't get weary in that. Don't think God has forgotten about you because He hasn't. He knows what He is doing. Also, when you are feeling lonely in your walk, turn to Him. Let Him assure you He is there and that He is your friend. I have found out over the years that God is an Oscar award winning God. He is the best actor in the world, and that Johnny Depp ain't got nothing on God. When we need a friend God can switch into the friend role for you. He will sit and sup with you like a friend. When we need a father or mother, God will come and embrace you as a parent would. He will also discipline you like a parent. God is here to be all we need Him to be, if we allow Him to be. We have to be open to listen to what He is saying to us.

I want to encourage you all to just embrace the change that will come upon your life, and not care what anybody has to say about what you are doing. There will be some that stick around and some that won't. The ones that won't stay, probably shouldn't have been there to begin with. People will get angry at you and make you feel like you are doing something wrong because you are trying to live for Christ and better your life. How does doing good make your life worse? It doesn't at all. The enemy will come in to confuse you and make you think you're going lose everyone around you that you care about, but he is a liar. Even if you were to lose them, God will restore you with more than what you had before and with real friends. Anyone that doesn't want to see you better yourself, isn't your friend. They don't want you to do better or know better. Misery loves company. If they are miserable and going through, then they don't want to hear about your God or how he is changing your life. They don't want to hear how happy you have been lately. As crazy at it may seem, people think they know more than God, and that they can save themselves from their own issues. Sooner or later, those will be the ones crying to you for help. It will be your duty to try and bring them into the light of Christ and out of Devil's darkness. Be strong in your weak areas. I strongly recommend you to get a spiritual mentor. This is someone who can call and check in on you and make sure you are doing ok and encourage you in your walk. A mentor can be a listening ear sometimes and to pray with you. When you finally start walking, you won't have all the answers and you won't do everything right. It's ok to fail, but as long as you repent and try not to make the same mistakes again. God will acknowledge your walk and he will see you and be proud. Also, if you do make the same mistakes again, God is so awesome that his grace extends beyond measure. He will still forgive you and throw your sins into the sea of forgetfulness. Please keep in mind, this is a day-to-day process. It won't happen overnight so don't get discouraged in what you can't do or can't say. In time, the Holy Spirit will touch you and you will be made new in Him. Sometimes, it pays to be the odd one that people talk about, because in the end your reward will be something they can talk about too. God honors a faithful one., If you will stand on His word and let the haters talk, God will shut their mouths up and make them come crawling apologizing and asking for forgiveness. Even they will see something different about you and they can see the hand of God showing up in your life. I have always felt like I was the odd one because I felt like I didn't fit in anywhere. I was the one always trying to make a name for myself because I wasn't comfortable just being me. I always hung out with older people. I felt like I got more out of being with them than I did with people my own age. Now I'm not saying that I didn't like every person I have come in contact who was my age. However my mind wasn't being stimulated like it was when I was with older people. I had to accept that I am different, a little odd, set aside and marked by Jesus Christ. I'm not going to look like everyone else. I'm not going to talk or walk like everyone else. I had to be ok with being me and know that God had me set aside for a time as this one. I couldn't be around all of the foolishness because it could have taken me down a path I may not have come back from. The devil more than likely would have taken me out. Don't fight against what God is doing in your life for the sake of some friends or whoever. It's not worth your soul going to hell. Align yourself under the will of God and watch him work in your life. Love yourself and know that you are beautiful despite what everyone else has said or didn't say. God made you and created you to his desire. In his eyes, you are perfect. Don't let anyone come and tell you otherwise.

CHAPTER 7

PROPHETIC RELEASE

Dear God, I come to you right now, just to say thank you for the lives you are touching, in this hour. Thank you for their ears being opened to hear and their hearts being ready to receive, God. I thank you for using me, your vessel, to share this message of Christ with your young women of God. I thank you for shaping them and molding them in your image. I thank you for every person that will pick this book up and read it, God. I thank you for giving them the desire to want to know you for themselves, and to build a relationship with you on a deeper level. Thank you for the victory that they shall and will have on today. God, you said that you will never put more on us that we can bear. I pray for strength in the name of Jesus. When things get tough, make them strong, God. When things aren't going how they see fit, let them know that you know all and see all, and that you have a plan. God, you might not come when we want you, but you're right on time. We thank you for the many blessings you will pour onto your people. God, I don't know every need but I pray that whatever their needs are, you will meet that need and much more. God, I thank you for the girl who is struggling in her self-esteem, I thank you for making her stronger now. Help her to see herself through you. Help her to understand her beauty in Christ, God. She is beautiful despite what the world tells her. If no one cares or loves on her, God, you care and you love her, on today. She is your daughter and you will never lead her astray. Touch her mind now in the name of Jesus. I take back every evil word that was said to lower her self-esteem and I take back every negative thought God, and I send it back to enemy's camp where it came from. Devil, you cannot have her life and you cannot have her esteem. Touch her right now God, in the name of Jesus. God, I pray right now for the girl who can't find herself after a loss or that feels abandoned by a parent. I pray that you would send direction into her life right now, in the name of Jesus. Send your light right now to shine on those dark places. I call depression to come forth and be sent back to the pits of Hell, in the name of Jesus. I call forth suicidal thoughts, right now, in the name of Jesus, and send them back to the pits of hell. I call forth the spirit of premature death and I send it back to the pits of hell. Devil, you don't win. You can't have our young daughters in the name of Jesus. I pray that you would be the father or mother in her life. Touch the places where she doesn't allow anyone in. Touch those places where she lays on her pillow and tears falls down. Touch those places that seem to always get the best of her and she feels the need to give in or give up. Let her know your hands are upon her right now

God. I pray for the girl that has been molested or raped, in the name of Jesus, I pray that you would do a surgery and go deep into the pain and rid her of the pain, in the name of Jesus. Touch the place where she feels unclean. Touch the place where she feels scared. Touch the place where she feels resentment, in the name of Jesus. Help her to be able to forgive. Give her joy, in the name of Jesus. God turn her situation around right now, in the name of Jesus. Make her whole in you. Touch her mind, rid her of the thoughts of lust, and premarital sex. Touch her and keep her covered right now. I pray that you will send her real friendships, in the name of Jesus. Send them someone that will encourage them, God, love them, and stand in the gap for them. Send someone who will not take and take from her, but give to her as well, God. Teach her how to be a friend, teach her how to build and keep relationships, in the name of Jesus. God, I pray for your light to be shown in them and that people may ask what I might do to be saved, oh God. God, I thank you for all that she shall go forth and do. God I thank you her education. Thank you for good grades; thank you for wisdom, in the name of Jesus. God I bind up every demon that might come to try and tear her down and tell her they can't do something. They can do all things through Christ that strengthens them. And we know our strength is in you and with you on our side who can be against us. Thank you for the lawyers, teachers, doctors, prophetess, pastors, preachers, leader's etc.

that you are raising up and that they will walk in. God, I declare that your daughter will be on fire for you. God, I pray that she will go chasing after you and your word. God, let her bring in their families and friends. God I thank you for revealing her callings and destinies in you God. I pray that you would shake up their ground. Go in and show the things you will have them to do and show her the things you will have her to say. Give her dreams and visions. Give her a greater anointing, in the name of Jesus. God, I declare that after today she will never be the same. Let her have a total transformation in you God. I just say thank you for all that you are doing right now and all that you will do in the future concerning your daughters. I declare these blessings upon your daughters right now, In the name of Jesus, I pray. AMEN!!

ABOUT THE AUTHOR

Born and raised on the West Side of Chicago, Ebony, attended Ella Flagg Young elementary school and graduated Grayslake North high school. She's the daughter of Valerie Hines and the late Lloyd James Steward. She's 25 and loves to have fun. She has a bright and bubbly personality, loves to laugh and make others laugh! She enjoys reading, writing, dancing and social outings. Ebony has five brothers, four living and one who preceded her in death.

Ebony is driven by her family, friends, God and the people God has called her to. She feels if she quits or gives up on her purpose that some young girl will miss her chance to be free or she would leave room for a young girl to not reach her full potential or get to know God. Her morals and values are also what drives her because she's always been taught to strive for greatness and to never settle. She's not satisfied with meeting the standard, Ebony wants to excel beyond the standard. Also, the need for change in this world drives her. The world today is in such a terrible place and she believes positivity is a necessity and if she could be a part of bringing change and positivity then she has to keep pressing.

Ebony, has faced more than her share of trials and tribulations. One thing that impacted her life greatly was the murder of her favorite cousin. She's survived bullying, peer pressure, rejection and low self-esteem. By the worlds labeling, she's considered a "statistic", but to her, she's a survivor. The devil intended to kill her and keep her stuck in a low place, but the moment she found God for herself, the power of the enemy was broken off her life. Now, she lives her life to tell of His goodness and to encourage young girls and women. Also, to encourage them to know Jesus as their Lord and Savior because without Him nothing is possible!

Ebony, is the founder of her non-profit mentoring group Facing the Mirror. She's a member of the prayer team and a youth leader at her church.

www.ingramcontent.com/pod-product-compliance
Lightning Source LLC
Chambersburg PA
CBHW062225080426
42734CB00010B/2032